The Power Of Or

Choosing And Doing What Matters Most

Joe Robert Thornton

VIZZIONNARY
PUBLISHING   BRANDS

The Chapters

The Power Of Or is based on my experiences as a leader of people. In this book, I primarily focus on the pragmatic aspect of leadership—addressing choices and decisions sensibly and realistically in a way that is based on practical application rather than theoretical considerations. For many of us, this is how we must approach the day-to-day challenges of our personal life while leading through many choices, decisions, and priorities.

I dedicate this book to those who are in search of implementing a pragmatic approach in their professional and personal lives and simplifying their lives to spend time doing what matters most.

Foreword

I knew that the timing was right for Joe to write this book. There are so many lessons Joe has learned in his professional career about balance, patience, discipline, self-discipline, decision-making, and prioritization.

Many of the lessons that Joe has learned in his professional career have come not as a result of being a leader of people, but instead from Joe being a father and husband. He has admittedly struggled at times with balance as he prioritized his professional life over his personal responsibilities in the early years of his career. While that focus helped Joe accelerate his career, it left him less than complete in his personal life.

Joe realizes that many leaders, who are growing in their professional careers, are challenged with this dilemma and that many of them are making tradeoffs every day.

Tradeoffs are an essential part of choices, decision-making, and priorities, but Joe has recognized that it is necessary to understand the impact of those tradeoffs in the moment as well as long-term. He has gained a deeper understanding of the consequences related to tradeoffs and shares his perspectives in this book.

There are many pitfalls related to the decisions that we make and what we decide to prioritize in our lives. Joe has heard many stories of regret from friends and colleagues about many of the tradeoffs they have made in their lives, and he is determined to help positively change that trajectory in the lives of others.

As Joe has continued to grow as a leader, I have been happy to see him apply these principles in his personal life. I believe they have made him a better person and a better leader.

When it comes to leadership and helping others, Joe believes that sharing his experiences are more powerful than sharing processes.

I have been able to observe the joy that Joe has gained from writing this book, and I am proud to see the result of his hard work shared with the world.

-Marie Cantu

Preface

We have entered a time in which the you-can-do-everything mentality has become the new normal.

In this book, I question whether we can do everything, but more importantly, I question *should* we do everything? And if we choose to attempt it, can we really do everything well.

I decided to write about the topics contained in this book based on my observations of what happens when we do not make good choices. They can lead to poor decisions, which can then lead us to prioritize the wrong things in our lives.

It was just as important for me to write about what it looks like when you make choices that benefit you and others around you, which can put your decision-making in alignment with who you are and what you want to accomplish. This can then lead you to spend time on what matters most in your life.

I have had many professional experiences of sitting in boardrooms, building annual operating plans and strategic plans. The business planning process can be a very harrowing experience, partially because of the schizophrenia of executive teams wanting to do everything... all at once. Writing this book is a way for me to help others approach this process in a more productive way.

The reality is that we are also constantly building personal plans and faced with the same challenge of attempting to do everything.

With the pace of life increasing, we face new challenges every day. For many of us, there is a level of capacity that can be unlocked to keep pace as we improve our competency personally and overall as leaders. However, there is also a limit. Knowing when that limit has been reached is one aspect of what the Power Of Or is all about.

There will be times in your personal and professional life in which And doesn't work—you must choose Or.

In other words, you cannot do everything that is in front of you—you must make choices to say yes to some things and no to others.

Part of the journey is understanding how great the need is to shift from And to Or, when we have reached capacity. Sometimes, it is self-inflicted as a result of our accepting work and responsibilities that we know we should not accept.

In the end, we are all forced to make many choices and decisions throughout our daily lives. Regardless of how we feel about the outcome of these choices and decisions, we can all be better at the process going forward versus where we are today.

To be most effective, each of us must find an approach that helps us positively impact those in our personal lives and those that we lead in our professional lives. In either case, we all have someone who is counting on us to make sound choices and decisions and prioritize those things that matter most in life.

In this book, I intentionally move back and forth between personal and professional growth. This is because it is challenging to be one person at home and show up at work and be a completely different person, especially when it comes to behaviors.

Many of the stories in this book are experiences based on my leadership journey. Many lessons have been learned about the power of choices, decision-making, and prioritization. Also, I present an account of my time watching how discipline was used or not used across multiple organizations and by many executive leaders. Every lesson has added valuable learning and has helped shape my leadership approach.

The Power Of Or explores pragmatic choices, decision-making, and prioritization and the real implications when we attempt to do it all. This book also explores the potential pitfalls in each area and offers some considerations which may help you in your daily life.

Lastly, this book is also about unlocking your reasonable ability to assess all choices, decisions, and priorities. Reasonable is the operative word given the fact that many of us make different choices when we are under duress. The closer we can align our decision-making during stressful times to look like our decisions during our greatest moments of clarity, the more satisfied we are likely to be with our decisions.

In reading this book, I hope that it improves your quality of life and ultimately, your leadership journey. On the business side, your people will thank you and likely so will your bottom line.

CHAPTER 1:

Moving From And To Or

There is a practicality to making a decision: making a decision is about making a choice. By making a choice, you choose a specific option. As a result of selecting that option, that means there is an option that you are not choosing.

Intentionally, this is a rudimentary approach, but one that is necessary to describe decision-making because it builds the basic understanding of The Power Of Or.

Occasionally, a new word or phrase shows up in the business world and injects itself into an organization. These words become part of daily conversations and become as much a part of the culture of the organization as do the vision, mission and guiding principles merely because they are spoken so often in meetings and in the halls between offices. These are called corporate buzzwords.

Perhaps "thinking outside of the box" is the all-time champion of corporate buzzwords followed by "paradigm shift." However, let's not forget the following: drill down, move the needle, at the end of the day, rightsizing, onboarding, cradle-to-grave, transparency, low-hanging fruit, and synergy. You may be nodding your head because you're a frequent user of these buzzwords or know someone that has fallen in love with these catchphrases.

There is more. Then along came sustainability, resilience, strategic agility, granular, and socialize. Even more recently, corporate buzzwords like ecosystem, core competencies, capability, ladder up, and all the way to bright seem to be parroted everywhere. Oh, I almost forgot one of the most frequently used buzzwords being spoken at this very moment across corporate boardrooms-value proposition.

I am curious as to why we feel so inclined to lose our personal, conversational identity and gravitate to this type of clichéd language.

If you have worked in a corporate office anywhere at any time, I am confident that these sound familiar to you and I'm sure there are many more corporate buzzwords floating around your office.

Often, these words or phrases come to life as a result of genuine, original thinking intended to stimulate new practices that improve the operation of the organization.

Without care, however, these words or phrases can quickly become overused and achieve buzzword status. The issue with this is that the word or phrase can become so distracting or tedious in conversation that it can minimize what is said next, and what is said next might be the vital thing that you wanted to be heard.

There is a single word that is unlikely to join this list of corporate catchphrases only because it is a common conjunction and has many other contextual uses in our daily conversations, though it accurately captures and communicates the dilemma challenging leaders today. That word is <u>And</u>.

However, this word has been part of one of the most overused catchphrases of the last decade or so, and that is "The Power Of And."

The Power Of And is creating anxiety, in business and in people's lives. I am not saying this for effect or to be melodramatic. We are attempting to do the impossible and asking others to do the impossible every day when we require multiple things to get done and, in the end, getting less than desirable results.

The challenging issues which business leaders face today—the new gig economy driven by businesses like UBER and Amazon, multi-generational workforces—from Baby Boomers to Generation Z, complex omni-channel development, record-low unemployment, and ever-changing brick-and-mortar dynamics, to name a few—cannot be easily solved. To that end, adding complicated strategies with the intent to take on every business headwind will only serve to heighten the business challenge ahead.

I was part of an operations strategy team years ago that brought in one of the largest consulting firms in the country to help us work on a store re-engineering project. The project was focused on solving... well, it doesn't even matter what the project was about. All that I remember about this project is that the principals for the consulting firm leading the project used the term, The Power Of And, about six thousand times during their presentations back to the executive team.

The phrase was so overused that it became a running joke. What was not funny about it was that some of our executive leaders began to buy into the idea of The Power Of And.

I suppose they bought into it partially due to the belief that the consultants, (considering the large sum of money that we were paying them), must know something that we did not know internally.

Candidly, I believe the executive buy-in to The Power Of And was also due to the hubris in our company at that time. We were brimming with self-confidence that everything we did would be successful and that we had the ability to do everything at once.

I'm confident that remembering an overused corporate catchphrase is not the legacy that this consulting firm wanted to leave with any of us, but that is precisely what I remember about the consulting engagement. In fact, that is the only thing that I remember about the consulting engagement.

I will acknowledge that the phrase, The Power Of And, makes sense in some dimensions of business. The Power Of And can be a way of stretching your thinking beyond your current state and getting more productivity out of your teams. The danger is that The Power Of And can lose its effectiveness when you realize that you cannot do everything at once.

Look, in our personal lives, we are faced with decisions every day in which we must choose—either which bill we can afford to pay when the total of our bills exceeds our income, which child's game or recital that we can attend when both activities are scheduled at the same time, etc.

We simply do not have the option of doing everything we wish to do in our personal lives.

That may sound pessimistic, but the reality is that we are constantly making tradeoffs... sometimes without even realizing it.

To that end, there must be a discipline of tradeoffs created in your organization that is parallel to the discipline you must manage in your personal life, especially considering the financial and human implications of business decisions.

By the way, tradeoffs can be good as it relates to discipline; however, tradeoffs can become a challenge when it comes to choices. I will discuss this in a later chapter.

I cannot tell you how many executive boardroom conversations I've been a part of over the years, since that store re-engineering consulting engagement, in which someone would talk about The Power Of And. The phrase was so overused that I could begin to predict the moment someone was going to use it. It was indeed buzzword bingo.

Again, I do believe that everyone that used the phrase, The Power Of And, had genuine intentions and thought that it was compelling. However, the most concerning aspect is that many of them believed that it was possible to achieve.

The Power Of Or is not meant to be an opposite approach to the Power Of And, just a different approach. Moving from And to Or is about changing your choices and decisions to change the outcome of the environment around you.

More specifically, the Power Of Or is about the delicate balance of having a clarity of purpose on what is important, what is not important, the ability to distinguish between the two, and then taking the appropriate action on those priorities to achieve the desired results — Choosing And Doing What Matters Most.

Rather than bog you down with a lot of processes to implement, I instead will focus on the practical aspect of choices, decision-making, and prioritization. The reason why?

I believe in the principle of leadership having two components- art and science.

The art of leadership is the subjective, expressive aspect that inspires people and drives culture. Without it, you may get compliance from your teams but likely not commitment. With the art of leadership, you can drive real talent development and become the model of culture that others outside of the organization attempt to replicate. It is also about pragmatism. The demonstration of realism and practicality can be strikingly relatable to your work force, mostly because this is how many of them are living every day. The best-in-class leaders, as it relates to the art of leadership, also understand the value of storytelling and using it to create a purpose for people doing the work they are being asked to do.

Let me emphasize one point here. At times, pragmatic leadership gets labeled as boring. However, being predictable, methodical and demonstrating a controlled temperament can be a powerful display of leadership mostly because it allows your people to stay focused on the work instead of on your mood as a leader. People in your organization will believe that you understand their plight. This understanding is key as it will prevent your messages from getting lost in translation because of unrealistic expectations and beliefs.

The science of leadership includes the objective, systematic, process-oriented aspects necessary to provide sound judgment for procedural continuity, formal training and development, and ultimately driving for results. Without the science of leadership, you may have great relationships, but you may also have a breakdown in consistency. You may never realize your full profit potential because of a lack of focus on financial stewardship and accountability. The best-in-class leaders, as it relates to the science of leadership, understand that financial success in the business unlocks the opportunity to invest in their people and their customers. They also understand that structure, measures, and processes allow for clarity that eliminates job frustration. People know where they stand and why.

Lastly, moving from And to Or is also about being decisive.

Taking forever to make a good decision is not necessarily better than making a quick, bad decision. The Power Of Or is about helping you to find that balance.

Moving from And to Or is just the beginning of the journey, but a foundation that is necessary to help you reach your full potential.

CHAPTER *2*:

The Root Of Discipline

There are many different definitions of discipline; however, most center around the same recurring words—terms like punishment, control, enforcement, instruction, rules, and obedience. In my opinion, all represent a negative view of the word discipline or, at the very least, not a positive or inspiring representation of the word.

The word included in the definition of discipline that seems to be referenced the least is self-control. At least Merriam-Webster recognizes it. I will come back to self-control.

Growing up, discipline was a word that I most often associated with the military. In part, this was because my stepfather served more than twenty years in the U.S. Army. As a result, we lived on a military base and I watched the regimented approach to all aspects of our lives play out on a daily basis—going to the grocery store which we called the PX (post exchange), passing by the barracks where the soldiers lived, watching the platoons performing exercises and hearing the constant sound of tanks shooting in the distance. You could set your watch by the tanks as they went off at the same time every morning. Everything related to the Army was done with precision and consistency.

Even at home, I'd watch my stepfather neatly press his uniforms and shine his shoes to a perfect gloss with the same level of precision week after week and year after year. I was also fascinated by the amount of practice that he dedicated to activities such as saluting. One day, I watched my stepfather salute more than a hundred times until he felt like he had demonstrated the perfect salute. That lifestyle was my exposure to discipline.

Because I grew up with these images in a military household, the association of the word discipline for me was aligned with control, rules, authority, obedience and the other synonyms that you will find listed in the dictionary. However, I believe many people not directly familiar with the military lifestyle growing up, would also make the same association of the word discipline.

This may be partly because of all the stereotypes about the military lifestyle portrayed on television and in movies. The image of soldiers awakened by a trumpeting officer at 5:00 a.m., soldiers marching in lockstep and being yelled at by a drill sergeant or a commander demanding the soldiers to drop to the ground and give him fifty push-ups are examples of discipline.

This is a stereotype of the military life, but perhaps a stereotype believed to have more truth than most others simply because the image has been pushed on us so often.

Nonetheless, in the military example, discipline can have a misguided, or at least a narrow definition. The definition of discipline is much more expansive than this. This brings me back to the other word in the description of discipline that seems to get very little focus.

Self-control.

For me, considering self-control in the definition of discipline completely changes the essence of the word and how it is defined. Self-control moves the ideology of the word from someone doing something to you and, if you don't comply, a negative consequence occurs, to the responsibility that you must make it happen because you want it to happen. That is self-control or as I will refer to interchangeably, self-discipline.

Discipline is also most often associated with something being difficult, infliction of pain by others, or even self-infliction. Perhaps, this is an overarching reason why discipline is portrayed in more of a negative light. After all, no one wants to be in pain or inflict pain on themselves.

Self-control is restraint exercised over your impulses, emotions, or desires. In a business setting, I believe that controlling your outward reaction is even more critical because your team is always watching how you react to situations and crises... always.

I believe that exercising self-control or self-discipline belongs in the highest echelon of behaviors of the best leaders, especially senior leaders.

The higher you go in an organization, and the fewer number of people that you need to answer to, the more critical is your level of self-control or self-discipline.

More critical, if for no other reason than the fact that your behavior can permeate the organization and, ultimately, can directly affect the morale, productivity, and results of the organization.

Because of this, to enact real discipline in your personal life or your organization, I believe that:

The root of discipline is self-discipline.

There are some basic tenets of discipline that we need to explore before discussing self-discipline.

On the professional side, in all my years of retail experience, I have rarely heard the word discipline used. As I think back over the years, even in my human resources role, about core competencies, leadership competencies, and other human resources processes, the word discipline never really showed up.

It is not to imply that other leaders did not believe that discipline was important; but I'm not sure that other leaders understood how important discipline is. This is not meant to be wordplay.

Perhaps I could describe it this way. I have heard leaders talk about culture and say that their mission, values, and guiding principles are "embedded" in their organization. Their culture is just the way that they live every day.

It is a statement that I have heard spoken but then it consistently went unchallenged. I mean, how are you supposed to respond to that? How can you dispute it?

I will say this. I cannot remember a time when anything important to me was "embedded." Instead, I emphasized *it*. I focused on *it*. I went to sleep thinking about *it* and I woke up thinking about *it*. I made it clear to everyone that *it* was a priority to me. I enacted discipline to ensure that *it* was always a priority. Saying that something is "embedded" is just code for it is not important, it is routine, or it is taken for granted- plain and simple.

Taking a passive approach to something that you are passionate about or believe deeply in is a confusing message. If *it* matters to you, everyone will know, and you will be known for *it*. That is how you respond to that.

So, back to discipline. It may have been implied, or "embedded," or there was a synonym for discipline represented in another competency listed, but discipline was not ever explicitly called out in any organization for which I have worked.

So, if discipline has not shown up as a specific focus area in my work environment, does that mean that discipline does not cut it as one of the most important skills to demonstrate? Well no, I don't see it that way—I simply see it as a competency that has not been demonstrated often enough for most organizations to realize the value.

There may be other needs that the organization prioritizes

ahead of discipline. I have had leaders share with me that they believe that discipline is only needed when times are difficult in the organization. That was eye-opening and far more honest than I would have expected to hear. I submit that if you do not demonstrate discipline in the best of times, you may be ill-equipped to demonstrate discipline when you need it, during the worst of times.

I feel strongly that discipline is mission-critical when it comes to organizational success. I have my own experience to prove that.

I was a regional-vice president for Starbucks Coffee Company in 2008 when the bottom fell out of the U.S. economy. At the time, I was responsible for 620 stores and 10,000 partners—which we called our employees at Starbucks.

Prior to 2008, if there was one company in America that did not "need" discipline, it was Starbucks. I say this with the understanding that all organizations need discipline, some to a lesser degree than others.

Starbucks had posted an unprecedented run of five percent or greater comparable store sales increase from the prior year- from the time of going public in 1992 to the run-up to the economic fallout in 2008. Most impressive—this occurred with Starbucks opening new store locations close to other existing Starbucks locations for most of the late 1990s and early 2000s. That was a staggering statistic then and even now.

Because of the massive store growth, there were plenty of satirical quips about Starbucks opening stores right next to one another. There was a comic strip that I recall at the time showing a Starbucks store opening inside of another Starbucks store. I had to laugh at that one.

In business, when we discuss the leaders of any industry, the word hubris often comes up. Some would say it is not arrogance if you can back it up, and Starbucks was talking the talk and walking the walk with their financial results in the early 2000s.

When I arrived at Starbucks in early 2006, I was able to enjoy a couple of years of significant growth before the signs of a slowdown began to show up. But when those signs did show up in 2008, they could not be ignored.

Of course, my view of the world when working for Starbucks was different from most people that had worked their way up and had already been there for many years. For those partners, there had never been a better time to be at Starbucks—that was all the time.

Howard Schultz, former Starbucks Chairman and CEO, would always say, "There has never been a better time to be at Starbucks." In fact, Howard said this at the first four meetings that I attended in 2006 and 2007. Of course, I must admit that at first, I thought he was being disingenuous and then I realized by the fourth meeting, that he really meant it—every time.

Before joining Starbucks, I'd spent fourteen years working for Blockbuster Video. This was a company that had an incredible run of its own and plenty of hubris, albeit a much shorter length of greatness. However, at their height of popularity, a cult-like following allowed Blockbuster to have a virtual lock on American entertainment. This was proven by the record numbers of people walking in on Friday and Saturday nights to rent movies from the late 1980s into the early 2000s.

Blockbuster, of course, faced its own precipitous drop in business around the end of 2002 as new technologies began to emerge. While they attempted to evolve the brand through technology, the threats were coming in many different forms and coming quickly. It was an interesting case study—a topic for another book. I will tease this—the demise of Blockbuster had nothing to do with Redbox or Netflix.

The point here is that I came from a company that, from a sales perspective, was fighting for its life every day for the last few years that I worked there. Even now, when I hear people talk about 2008 and their version of tough business times, I recount my Blockbuster days.

The Blockbuster elevator was going down, and the Starbucks elevator was shooting up.

The second point was that, despite all the business troubles facing Blockbuster, our hubris was still pervasive, and we were still not demonstrating discipline, even though it was needed. It was an exhausting time and an exhausting experience.

So, arriving at Starbucks to work in 2006 was great for me for a whole host of reasons that most could not understand or appreciate unless they had been on a ship like Blockbuster that was sinking faster than the Titanic. My apologies for the movie reference... but you should have seen that one coming.

It was now 2008 at Starbucks and things were changing, and not for the better.

According to the National Retail Federation, annual retail sales growth in the United States went from a positive three percent comparable sales in 2007, down to almost negative four percent comparable sales in early 2009. Starbucks was faced with an even steeper challenge. Compared to the NRF report, Starbucks had been tracking at a higher positive comparable sales versus the NRF report in 2007 and then fell precipitously off to a more negative comparable sales figure versus the NRF report in early 2009.

Of course, when you look at it logically, it should not have been a surprise to us. It stands to reason that families looked at their budget, and other than selling timeshares, Starbucks might have been the first casualty on their list. A five-dollar-a-day habit no longer made sense in the new world order of 2009.

As a previous president of U.S. retail for Starbucks at that time would describe it: "we were sliding down a mountain and trying to find something to grasp onto." It was a sobering image, but as fitting as any that I recall at that time.

So, where is this story heading? Back to where we started and what we had to do at Starbucks as a result of the situation at that time.

What we had to get right at Starbucks in 2009 was discipline, specifically operational discipline. It may not have been a dire need in 2006 when I came on board, but it was clearly needed now in 2009. The operational playbook had to change.

Of course, Howard Schultz had returned as CEO in 2008 to restore the culture of the company. That story is well-documented and as important as any to the history of the company. Going into 2009, though, it was about more than just culture, and we could not save our way to prosperity—it had to be about operational execution. It had to be about choices, decisions, prioritization and ultimately discipline... and each of them would pose their challenges.

We made some progress, but candidly, we stumbled through 2009, as most companies did.

We had minimal internal experience to deal with this type of situation. Most of our senior field leaders and executive leaders had been with Starbucks for some time and, frankly, had experienced only good times. Even those who came from other organizations years earlier could not recount a business challenge on a scale that looked anything like 2008.

For me, it was a bit more relative, and I could say that I had seen worse because I had. I am certainly not going to minimize the challenge that we faced at Starbucks. It was as real as real gets. However, coming from Blockbuster, every year from 2002 to 2006 felt like and operated like 2008. How is that for perspective? After the Blockbuster experience of the final few years, I had the opposite of hubris. Let's see, what would I call that? How about paranoia.

Arriving at Starbucks in 2006, I felt like any day it could all be taken away, even when I was operating a region at almost double-digit comparable sales. All had changed by 2008.

On the operational side of the business, I could see the opportunity clearly, very clearly.

As a team, we focused on putting processes in place. We went through the rigor of identifying key metrics. This was about taking every measurement that was focused on across all departments and categories of business that showed up in the stores. We identified thirty-seven key metrics.

We then had to enact discipline by agreeing that all things cannot be equal and had to determine the most critical key metrics to the actual success of the business. With plenty of gnashing of teeth, we reduced it to twelve key metrics. We also worked on producing a stop-light scorecard showing red, yellow and green status, pulling the field focus toward profit and loss report reviews and implementing a cadence by which to use these tools on a monthly basis.

We did not add any new tools—just a focus on the ones that we already had and a disciplined way to utilize them.

With the construct in place in 2009, by the beginning of 2010, we were demonstrating a repeatable routine of discipline that had not been present before the economic collapse.

Starting in 2010, we visited stores with a laser-like focus. We looked at three pieces of paper. The one-page scorecard which contained the twelve key metrics—with goals and results, and the two-page profit and loss statement, the front page with sales and revenues and the second page with expenses and profits.

It may seem like I'm oversimplifying this, but that is all we did in 2010 and 2011. We had to.

We also tapped into the discipline that we observed from store managers. We shared more best practices than we had before the economic crash. Whether it was a store manager in Fort Worth, Texas with her maniacal focus on drive-thru speed of service, or a manager in Los Angeles reconfiguring his store to sell an insane number of frappuccinos, or a manager in Austin, Texas who did interviews at 5:00 a.m. for people that she needed to hire to open the store at that hour every day. Her approach was simple—if they didn't show up for the interview on time at 5:00 a.m., there was little confidence on her part that they would be reliable and make it to work on time when scheduled to open the store at 5:00 a.m. — just common sense.

There were hundreds of these types of best practices that we leveraged across the region and shared across the country.

We didn't "reinvent the wheel" or "boil the ocean"- I should have mentioned those when I was discussing corporate buzzwords. Oh well.

Instead, we put routines in place, and we followed them and expected everyone to follow them. We rewarded people who followed them and achieved the desired results. It sounds easy, right? You may be surprised by my response to this question—yes, it was easy.

It was discipline on a massive scale. My 620 stores and the 10,000 employees in the region were all marching in the same direction. I am confident that discipline can be accomplished on any scale, but the vision, the mission, the measures and the inspiration to do it has to be in place.

One other point to share on this:

A quote from "Onward" in 2012, a book written by Howard Schultz: "Starbuck's transformation was being achieved not simply because we were effectively responding to external economic, technological, and social challenges, or correcting problems we had brought upon ourselves. Rather, it was being achieved because of how partners tried to solve these problems."

That is precisely what happened.

Discipline requires leadership.

From that time on, when I heard executives in any organization talk about how difficult it is to make a significant change and make it quickly in a large organization, I would call bullshit.

It just takes discipline.

So, if discipline works and it is so essential to organizational success, then why is there such a lack of it?

Sometimes we create barriers that prevent us from getting to true discipline... self-inflicted wounds.

Many organizations are plagued by leaders who say irresponsible things like, they need to: "raise the bar" and "drive capability" and "increase bandwidth" and all the other nonsensical statements made with reckless abandon.

When you allow these statements to become part of your culture, and no one in the organization pushes back or challenges to ensure that discipline is in place to balance this, most of the teams will put forth the effort to do it all with little regard of the consequences for themselves or the organization.

This scenario is perhaps the most dangerous aspect when discipline is not in place. The impact on morale can be far-reaching and irreversible. The feeling of nothing-is-good-enough and a sense of failure can blanket the organization.

Lack of discipline is perhaps the one act of senior leaders that can drive a wedge between them and their workforce quicker than anything else.

What I have learned is that the lack of discipline is everywhere.

For example, I recently had dinner at a prominent restaurant chain that is known for having a rather lengthy menu. Too many pages to count, but for sure more than two hundred selections on the menu and at least eighty of them were just for chicken! I am confident that I skipped several pages as I scrolled through the menu with the disdain of a required reading assignment in high school.

If you could dream it, they had it on the menu.

As I looked deeper into the menu, everything on the menu made sense for them to carry, as all the different options catered to a group that, without those options present, might not frequent the restaurant. That said, I must admit that I'm a bit suspicious of a restaurant that is trying to be all things to all people. I am not sure that any restaurant can excel at cooking so many different types of food.

Putting my personal feelings aside and putting on my business hat, my takeaway is that there must be many items on the menu potentially causing the organization to lose money based on the lack of velocity. For those low-selling items, the business needs to stock the ingredients... just in case that one person orders it. There was no way for me to know how many low selling items were on their menu, but I do know that, by force rank, you will always have lower selling items.

In business, you must balance the needs and wants of the customer against the costs of managing the business. I am not saying that the customer is not the most critical stakeholder in decisions made about the business. It is tricky, but in this example, a customer won't know what they're not missing if the item is never introduced into the menu.

Of course, the perspective that has been shared from inside of this organization is entirely different. They believe that getting people talking about their extensive menu drives incremental sales. That may well be true, to a point. It could also be at the expense of profitability.

The fundamental issue in my perspective regarding this restaurant is a lack of discipline somewhere in the organization to make the tough decision. The discipline to declare that there is a finite number of items that we should have or can specialize in on the menu before there comes a point of diminishing returns.

On some level, the issue has nothing to do with dollars and cents. It is the consideration of the pressure placed on the supply chain, the marketing team, the operations team, and the back-of-house cooks themselves that can become overwhelming... and it is all self-inflicted.

And yet, in spite of all this effort, there may not even be a financial benefit to carrying all the items that are on the menu.

Now you could present the hypothesis, in this example, that removing items from the menu would negatively impact sales. To that I would say, it depends. It is possible that removing an item from the menu could mean that the same customer finds a new favorite and sales stay the same. Instead, I would recommend that you work the equation from the other end. Consider whether the items actually produce sales at all from customers perusing the menu—factoring in cannibalization of other items.

Beyond the Xs and Os of whether the business made money due to the incremental items, there becomes a responsibility of the leaders to recognize that there is a lack of discipline in place. However, it should also be the responsibility of everyone in the organization to speak up, especially if they feel that there is an overloaded expectation that cannot be delivered effectively.

It gets to this point:

When there are challenges in business, the burden of responsibility, whether disproportionately or appropriately placed upon the leader, cannot be solely the leader's responsibility.

Notwithstanding, the meal was excellent!

Unfortunately, my restaurant experience was not unique as it was reinforced by yet another experience the very next day.

I made a trip to the grocery store—yes, I still actually go to the grocery store, just not as frequently as I used to as our world continues to evolve.

My experience that stood out on this trip to the store was realizing the proliferation of items that are present down each aisle. One example was the staggering number of choices of peanut butter that exist—even within the same brand. Perhaps, I was more surprised than I should have been by my experience because it had been quite some time since I'd purchased peanut butter.

This national brand was well-represented with different options-Creamy, Extra-Crunchy, Reduced-Fat, Omega 3, Natural Creamy, and Natural Honey Creamy. Each with different colored lids and slightly different wording on the labels. What I thought would be and should be one of my easiest decisions of the day left me standing in the peanut butter section for far too long.

I began to feel a level of pressure, as though time was about to expire for me to make my selection. I was there so long that I looked around to see if anyone was watching me. I found no one else was in the aisle—clearly, no one knew or cared about my self-imposed dilemma regarding peanut butter. The experience left me questioning my ability to make simple decisions.

I had another experience on the very next aisle selecting refried beans. There I was attempting to choose between Traditional, Vegetarian, Spicy-Jalapeno, No-Fat, and Low Sodium. Again, all with very similar labels, making the choice that much more difficult. While standing there, I reflected on how difficult these decisions have become. I am sure that many years ago, the options were much more streamlined by product segment, especially when it comes to peanut butter and refried beans.

I am confident that there is research in the case of the refried beans that adding another flavor or option would potentially grow the overall sales of the category. If the traditional refried beans sold twelve units per store per week and then the new varieties of refried beans sold an additional three units each per store per week; then this seems like a very logical decision to make in adding varieties. What must be proven is whether the incrementality is enough to offset the additional costs and understanding a calculation of cannibalization—the number of customers that moved from traditional refried beans to one of the new options. This is all a part of business discipline.

I am not suggesting that organizations don't take the time to go through this exercise with all innovation. What I am suggesting is that you can make any number lead you to the conclusion that you want. If you are determined to increase the selection to drive incrementality, you can do that at the expense of eroding margin and adding potentially unjustifiable costs. If you are going to enact discipline by limiting the number of items, and have the rigor in place to do so, that decision will drive you to a different outcome.

These examples stuck with me for all the apparent reasons related to discipline. These examples also stayed top-of-mind because I arrived back home with a different jar of peanut butter and a different can of refried beans from what I intended to purchase. Not only were my decisions made difficult by having so many options, but the proliferation of possibilities also confused me and caused me to be dissatisfied due to choosing the wrong items.

I know that these two examples may seem trivial in the scheme of all the decisions that we make throughout our day. But I share all of this to emphasize that discipline or lack of discipline permeates every part of business and every aspect of our daily lives—even in the small decisions.

We have become accustomed to so many more options in all that we do that it has become our new normal. The risk of anything in your life becoming your normal mode is that it becomes your routine. That can be a good-for-you routine or a bad-for-you routine.

With so many of our choices, decisions, and priorities impacted by discipline or lack of it, it is vital to get good-for-you routines in place in this part of your life and leadership journey.

As a leader, I believe that you have the responsibility to create discipline in your organization up, down and across. Your people are counting on you to do it... even when they don't know that is what they need.

I also believe that discipline begins where most improvement begins—with us looking into the mirror. It begins with self-discipline.

CHAPTER *3:*

Self-Discipline

Let's get into self-discipline.

When I began to research the word discipline, one interesting point is that most of the techniques that were written about in articles and books focused excessively on discipline related to children. In fact, there were very in-depth approaches to helping children be more disciplined. Many of these books and perspectives viewed discipline through the narrow, compliance-driven definition that I discussed at the beginning of the previous chapter.

Interestingly though, I did not find many articles written about discipline related to adults.

Most important, regarding this conversation, I found even less information about self-discipline and the application of it related to organizational success. I am certainly not implying that I'm the first to talk about the topic, but I was surprised at the limited amount of content available about it.

I want to re-emphasize a point that I discussed in the previous chapter.

While I believe that everyone has a responsibility to demonstrate self-discipline, I believe that leaders of people have an even greater responsibility to demonstrate it. If for no other reason, the higher you move up in an organization, there are fewer people to exact discipline on you as a leader. It then becomes an issue of self-discipline—you as a leader making tough decisions and tradeoffs with limited prompting or guidance.

We will talk more about how this ties into prioritization in a later chapter.

Self-discipline can be described in many ways.

Self-discipline is about excelling and staying focused on the task at hand regardless of your surroundings, even when things are not going well in your surroundings.

Self-discipline is also about doing the things you should do even when you do not want to do them. Because when we can choose between being focused and staying on track, (especially on a task that is not desirable), versus physical and material comfort, we will often choose the latter.

Self-discipline does not allow space for a wishy-washy approach either.

One of my mentors would always tell me this as clearly as anything I have ever heard, "Do not ever use these three words- Try, Think and Hope." She would go on to say, as I paraphrase, "You don't try to pick up a pen, you pick it up. You don't think you know something. You know it or you don't." And finally, she would always share, "Hope is not a strategy."

When you are demonstrating self-discipline, these words will disappear from your vocabulary.

Examples of self-discipline in our personal life are exercising without the need to hire a personal trainer, eating healthy without the need to start the latest fad diet, and paying bills that we must pay before spending money on things that we want.

Self-discipline, when demonstrated, can also increase our level of responsibility.

Think about the example of a personal trainer. When you sign up for a gym membership and hire a personal trainer, of course you have good intentions. However, if you spend the next three months working out, and see no progress in your results, it makes it easier and probably likely to blame the trainer for not pushing you hard enough. You have absolved yourself from the situation—no self-discipline and no responsibility for the outcome, a double-negative.

In the end, you have lost money, you have lost time, you did not accomplish the goal that you set out to achieve, and it is even someone else's fault. What a prime example of how difficult and, at the same time, how important self-discipline can be. That leads to this belief:

Self-discipline cannot be delegated.

Going to the gym is an example to which many of us can relate. According to quora.com, 80% of people who sign up at a gym as part of their New Year's resolution in January have dropped out by the second week of February. There are a whole host of reasons for that, most of those reasons cleverly disguised as excuses. It's a staggering statistic for sure. It is a clear sign that the basis for making the decision was not reinforced with a real commitment to self-discipline. What is most surprising is that this statistic looks the same year after year.

Examples of self-discipline in our professional lives are sometimes as simple as being on time, even if there is no expectation of being punctual or even if no one else is ever on time, meeting deadlines and planning your time accordingly for that to happen, and steering clear of office gossip. This is self-discipline that is relatively easy and completely controllable.

Self-discipline, though, can be fraught with excuses.

Let's focus on self-discipline and the impact on decision-making.

Every day, we make many decisions. Self-discipline is the ability to help us make smart decisions, and not only the most comfortable choices.

One of the essential steps to aid in self-discipline is to remove all temptation from your environment. Here's an example that likely resonates with many of you: controlling what you eat. If you stock your pantry with junk food, there is a much higher probability that you will consume more junk food than you would if those items were not in your pantry and you had to utilize more effort to go out and purchase them from the store. In controlling what you eat, if the temptation is present, your willpower may not be strong enough to resist it. Counting on willpower to offset temptation is a trap that many of us have fallen into.

It is important to note that self-discipline is not the same as willpower.

Self-discipline is the precursor to willpower. Self-discipline is not allowing the temptation to enter the situation, which would then create the need for willpower.

There are many reasons that many of us fail when it comes to willpower. One is the simple truth that many believe that we have the necessary willpower to reject temptation. That's okay, though—we are all born with the same internal challenge. The fundamental question to consider is how you got into a situation in which temptation and willpower are battling for control. It likely has much more to do with a lack of self-discipline than it does with a lack of willpower.

Unfortunately, we aren't born with self-discipline. The good news is that it is a learned behavior so everybody can attain it.

Self-discipline requires motivation, and real motivation usually comes from within. I may be repetitive in saying this, but with intention, self-discipline is hard.

Lastly, the effort and focus that self-discipline requires can be draining. Of course, when you begin to take ownership of your discipline, it can be so much easier at times to give in to the temptation and hope maybe to get it right the next time. We usually know what happens when we take that approach. It is called forming a bad habit.

As it relates to leadership, the implications of self-discipline are different—people are counting on you to demonstrate self-discipline.

Self-discipline will be vital when you are in a decision-making leadership position and are faced with "The Power Of And" in your business. It will happen at some point in your career— you will be given a more significant workload than you can manage. Your choices, your decisions, your prioritization will be challenged.

I worked alongside a leader who demonstrated the strongest self-discipline in his personal life of anyone that I'd met—a guy named Alex. Alex was in a vice-president role at the time, doing the same job that I was doing. Alex was disciplined about what he ate, what time he went to bed, and going to the gym consistently. When he traveled, he called home every night at the same time. His routines were impressive in every way and frankly, something that I envied.

On the business side, I also observed Alex model great self-discipline. Alex was able to demonstrate consistency in how he set up his day and how he adjusted for unexpected situations that are part of business.

The most impressive aspect to me about Alex's discipline was that I never saw him get frustrated when the unexpected situations occurred. He would allocate time for the situation, and once it was resolved, he would then reallocate his time for the balance of the day, ensuring that he met all the commitments he had made for that day.

Of course, this all seems logical until your first interruption of the day occurs. I've witnessed many leaders who could not get back on track after a crisis occurred in their day—not tactically and sometimes not emotionally.

But here was Alex. Always responding and adjusting. After observing Alex for more than a year, we had dinner one night and, at that point, I felt comfortable in my role and comfortable enough in our relationship to ask him questions about self-discipline.

Frankly, I did not feel very self-disciplined at that time in my life, either personally or professionally. I knew what I had to do in my personal experience related to self-discipline and I wasn't doing it, so I wasn't going to bore Alex with that.

Instead, being newer in the role than Alex, I needed to focus on how to be more efficient at the job. I have always believed that no one understands the role that you have like someone who is in the role that you have, so Alex was the best source that I could tap into regarding my questions.

So, the obvious first question that I posed to Alex was, "How do you do it all?" as I helplessly raised my hands to the sky. To my surprise, Alex had a very perplexed look on his face. I realized, in that moment, that Alex's self-discipline routines were so routine he didn't understand what I was asking him.

I repositioned the question to, "How do you stay so disciplined in your personal and professional life? I never see you miss a beat and frankly, you make it look easy."

I could tell that this question got through and I could see Alex preparing to answer the question before I even finished asking it.

Alex was very forthright in his response. He said, "First, none of this is easy. Frankly, I drive my wife and my kids crazy with so much thoughtful planning." Alex went on to say, "My family has come to understand that if I don't do this, I won't be able to maximize the time that we spend together and still make time for myself to make sure that I am best prepared to take on the challenges of each day, and of course, to be successful at work."

That all sounded great and made perfect sense, but it did not get to the matter of how, so I pressed on. I also asked Alex about what happened when he couldn't get everything done. Alex was again very calculated and matter-of-fact with his answer. He said, "That's easy; I simply don't do the things that don't matter." Regardless of the conviction in his voice I was not going to allow this canned answer to slip by.

I replied, "I mean, how do you know that it wasn't important? Surely you must have items on your list to do daily that you don't get to even though you wanted to." Alex responded, "Of course I do, but that next thing wasn't as important as the last thing I accomplished that day, so it either moved to the next day, or it disappeared."

While I was learning valuable lessons from the conversation, I found myself almost frustrated that I couldn't get Alex to crack and at least get to enjoy the satisfaction of a "gotcha" moment in response to any one of the questions I asked. I know, that wasn't a healthy thought, but hey, I'm human too.

Alex continued over the next hour to weave a story of true self-discipline. It all started with personal self-discipline and flowed into professional. If there was going to be a gap in self-discipline, Alex said that it needed to occur with him personally because that only affects him. The impact of having a gap in self-discipline towards his family or in his leadership role, caused too many ripples, ones from which it could be difficult to recover.

I asked Alex to share an example of what he meant related to his self-discipline. Alex quipped, "That's easy—I might have to skip a workout at the gym to take my son to baseball practice or to take a last-minute conference call. The implications of putting my workout first would have a negative impact on my son or the business due to my need to catch up on what I'd missed."

Nothing Alex said over dinner was foreign to me, but it was the level of conviction with which he said it that left a lasting impression. He meant it, and he was living it.

There are elements from that conversation many years ago that I still apply in my daily life. Again, proof that, while we are not born with self-discipline, any of us can learn to be self-disciplined.

With self-discipline in place, you make better choices, you make better decisions, you simplify your life, and ultimately, you become better at prioritization.

The good news is this:

When self-discipline is in place, you begin to change And into Or.

Let's talk more about why it is important to change And into Or.

CHAPTER 4:

'And' Is A Four-Letter Word

If you grew up as I did, you might be familiar with the term "four-letter word." While the term four-letter word is typically associated with coarse or offensive language, there are many such words that show up in organizations that, while not explicit, can be damaging. In every book, I will dedicate a chapter to a four-letter word.

In this book, that word is **And.** I believe that And can create significant damage in your personal life when you attempt to do everything. Moreover, in a leadership role impacting many more people, And can create havoc inside of any organization. The word comes with many risks. One of those is:

The word And draws a direct line to multitasking.

Honestly, I could have just titled this chapter multitasking, but there are many other environmental elements that lead us to the place of multitasking that must be understood as well, starting with today's business environment.

Today, there is a different perspective about business. An expectation, almost approaching a requirement, to do everything and believe that it is possible to do everything effectively.

There is also a belief that, with time, business has become more complex, requiring different skill sets, including the ability to multitask.

What I will say about that is this... the fundamentals of business and the business-to-customer functional relationships have not changed since the beginning of formalized business models. Perhaps the payment methods, the delivery methods and things like the expectation of speed have changed, but what people want and what a business provides in a B2C (business-to-customer) relationship has remained relatively unchanged. Where it has changed, business has appropriately adjusted to match the demands of what is new and changing in our daily lives, mostly driven by technology.

The complexity and speed of the world around us does not make a strong enough case for the multitasking that occurs in our lives every day. Additionally, the fast-paced business environment does not make a strong enough case for organizations endorsing irresponsible multitasking. This can result in leadership teams walking out of the boardroom with strategic plans and operating plans the size of War And Peace, calling for their teams to do everything at once.

The And Strategy is about putting all the priorities on the table, sorting them, and figuring out how to accomplish all of them without the thought of limiting the priorities. It is not uncommon for senior leadership to believe that their people can get more work done than what they themselves believe they can accomplish. In a fundamental sense, it is admirable. It may even be aspirational. However, it is not realistic. The words capacity and capability also get many organizations into trouble with their people—I will discuss that later in the book.

And is the keyword in the catchphrase, The Power Of And. As it is uttered in many boardrooms, The Power Of And is a theoretical approach. I describe it as merely speculative because numerous studies debunk the belief that you can effectively do multiple things at once and certainly not all things at once, without losing productivity.

To go further, I believe that And is a liability in any organization, particularly as it relates to setting up your vision, making strategic decisions, aligning priorities, and ultimately, the tactics to deliver on your strategic expectations.

Conversely, The Power Of Or is true leadership decision-making. It is being clear about what is most important, telling everyone what the priorities are and aligning your team and their work against it.

The Power Of Or is also about ensuring that all other things are identified as less important. This callout of non-essential work is key because your teams may still attempt to do it all on the remote chance that you may ask them about a priority that was left as ambiguous.

The Power Of Or allows you to liberate yourself from the

overwhelming burden of doing everything—many of those things not being important anyway. We owe it to ourselves in our personal lives, we owe it to ourselves as leaders, and ultimately, we owe it to the people that we lead.

So back to And. Let's talk about it and its relationship to multitasking. To re-emphasize the point, I believe that:

The word And draws a direct line to multitasking.

If there is only one thing that you take from this book and apply to your daily life, it is to eliminate multitasking.

Interestingly, the word multitasking did not even exist until a 1965 IBM published report praised the capabilities of its latest computer. Imagine how simpler life was then compared to now—not necessarily simpler in world challenges, but simple in relation to our available choices.

There are many studies about the unproductive aspects of multitasking, and yet, we have created generations of people that genuinely believe they are more effective when multitasking, sometimes even thriving. Today, people wear the word multitasking like a badge of honor, believing that it is better to be busy with all things than to be great at one thing.

Research has shown that only about two percent of the population are super multitaskers—it is a genetic gift. These people are genuinely able to do several different activities at the same time without losing efficiency or losing quality as they do their work. Perhaps, it is less important to focus on how or why, as the rest of us cannot learn this rare gift.

Instead of focusing on whether you are in that two percent group, focus on what you can do to reduce the multitasking that is robbing precious hours from your life. That is correct—you are not saving time by multitasking—you are losing time.

Listen, most of us believe that we are great drivers. The statistics available from the Department of Transportation, based on vehicle accident data, would prove that many of us are generous in our self-assessment. Perhaps, we would be better drivers if we weren't distracted drivers. You can begin to see a pattern here—many matters link back to multitasking.

In fact, believing that we are good at something almost invites multitasking.

With multitasking, we quickly associate that, if there are two things that we are good at, then we will be equally as good at both while doing them simultaneously.

This explains why we sometimes attempt to text while we are driving. Inherently, we know that driving and texting at the same time is not a good idea. Either our attention to driving is diminished, or our texting experience is a bit challenged or both.

Multitasking while driving is more dangerous because driving requires all your attention due to the unpredictable nature of those around you, especially when those around you could be multitasking as well. It has been reported in surveys that fifty-nine percent of adults, young and old, admit to using their phones while driving. Maybe the question that must be asked first is how many people tell the truth in surveys? Well, if it is not one hundred percent that tell the truth, then assume that the texting and driving number is higher than fifty-nine percent. Nonetheless, we continue with multitasking behind the wheel.

Again, most of us, that would be ninety-eight percent, do not have the gift of productive multitasking.

Besides, recent neuroscience research tells us that the brain does not do two tasks at the same time as we believe it does. Instead, the brain switches quickly from one task to another so suddenly, at times, that we do not notice it. Each time we move from one activity to another, there is a stop and start process that occurs in the brain.

This start-stop-start again process is complicated and time-consuming. Rather than saving time, it costs us time. In the end, we are less efficient, we make more mistakes, and over time it can zap our energy. This is the energy that we will need as the day progresses.

Our brain multitasking is not nearly as good as we think that it is. You can be engaged in an activity on the left side of your brain—something creative—and begin an activity on the right side of your brain, let's say something more logical or practical.

You are not doing both activities at the same time. In fact, you are now diverting your attention from one part of your brain to another part of your brain. That takes time, that takes resources, that takes brain cells. Brain cells that you will wish you had later in the day.

During this process, it is almost impossible to notice, but you are probably slower and not nearly as good at doing both activities at the same time. If you are used to doing two things at a time, you can become conditioned to considering that to be your new norm and therefore, not realize that you are slowing yourself down. It is a lot to think about, but mostly, it is a lot to admit to.

The good news is that we can shift our focus quickly. Sometimes, it takes just a fraction of a second. The time used is not as critical as the bandwidth that the brain requires to move back and forth. Even if you make the switch quickly and use the smallest of incremental time, it still may affect your performance, and it may also affect the quality of the work that you ultimately produce.

None of this would be an issue if the human brain, as complex as it is, could transition effortlessly from one job to the next, but it cannot. Multitasking forces you to pay a mental price each time you stop one task and start another.

The myth of multitasking is that it will make you more productive. The laser focus on one thing is what actually makes you more productive.

I know, it feels like I am belaboring this point about multitasking—I am. Allow me to belabor a bit more.

Let's talk about our smartphones. Not only do smartphones provide unprecedented access to information, but they also offer unparalleled opportunities to multitask. Any activity can be accompanied by or, perhaps better stated, interrupted by music, search engine headlines, or social media updates. Any one of these activities can derail you for seconds, minutes, or hours.

We have so many distractions with our smartphones that we no longer even identify them as distractions.

Understanding how the brain works and why we find multitasking so appealing will help you realize the hazard of pulling out your smartphone over and over throughout the day.

Multitasking feels like we are doing two things simultaneously, so the danger lies in asking one mental process to do two incompatible things. Many of us cannot do two simple things at the same time, like rub our stomach and pat our head. For those that can, it still involves a conscious effort to do so. Think about how simple it is when asked to do either one of those separately.

This is not the same as when you are on a conference call at work and the agenda item being discussed is irrelevant to you, so you go ahead and answer email. This is a much more obvious disconnection from one activity to take on another. You may not realize until later that you missed something which was discussed on the call because your attention was diverted to reading or responding to emails.

This is still an issue, but it does not appear to pose the same danger as driving and texting, so we are more inclined to do it and believe that the risk is very low. It may in fact be a low physical risk, but not necessarily a low mental risk.

This overconfidence that we have in our ability to multitask extends to other parts of our lives.

A recent survey showed that many students who use social media, text, or watch television while studying, believe that they can still comprehend the material they're studying.

After all, they are Generation Z—for many of them this has been their normal behavior growing up. It could be true that those students are still effective with their classwork… but to a point. The student who multitasks while studying could be a straight-A student. Well, that makes it difficult for their parents to argue with their child's logic. Except to say this- without the distractions, perhaps the straight-A student, instead of being 17th in their class, would have been valedictorian.

I know, good luck getting that point across to your child. The point here is that there is a diminished level of skill and execution when two activities are attempted at the same time. No matter where your skill level is at, multitasking will diminish it further.

This confidence is especially understandable for very simple tasks like studying. Everyone knows texting behind the wheel is dangerous but listening to music while studying seems harmless. Listening to music while doing almost anything seems harmless. However, both activities can negatively impact your ability to drive.

That may not be relatable to all of you, but consider this—have you ever turned down the radio or quieted passengers when you were driving, and a heavy downpour occurred, or you were driving on an icy road? How about when you were looking for an address? You may have felt as if you could concentrate better without the distraction of music or other voices. Okay, maybe this has only occurred with the older generation or it is quite possible that many of you are laughing right now as you are reading this.

The real challenge is that many people multitask solely because they see no harm in it; others perceive that there are actual benefits to doing so. They say they multitask to save time and to be more efficient, not less. Wow, there is a huge disconnect here.

Music, likely the most common culprit of multitasking, is added to tasks because many people have said that it makes them feel relaxed, making it easier to manage a task that will require their presence for an extended period.

Even if you fully appreciate the mental impact, you might tolerate that in exchange for the perceived benefit that you are getting from the music.

Attempting to watch a movie, assuming it is a movie that you have not seen before, and texting is not impossible to do. However, in the seven seconds that you looked away to text, you might have missed the most crucial clue in the movie as the lead actress threw a letter opener in the trash that ended up being the murder weapon. I am just saying—is it worth it? No matter how good you believe that you are at multitasking, you are going to miss something. You had better hope that what you missed was not important.

So next time you think you are multitasking, stop and be aware that you are switch-tasking. Then give yourself a time limit and focus on just one task and see if you can't complete it better, faster, and with less energy.

To be clear, we can do two tasks at a time. What is impossible is truly concentrating on more than one task at a time.

So, eliminating multitasking is a critical element on this journey to remove "And" and replace it with "Or." I repeat, multitasking is an activity that we can impose on ourselves and often do, believing that we can do more than one thing at a time. Back to this point:

Multitasking is the constant activity of switching tasks. Multitasking takes additional time that we have not accounted for, and it impacts the quality of the tasks.

Still not convinced of the impact of multitasking?

I recommend that you take a small test that I learned about recently. It is from a group out of Denmark called the Potential Project.

- Start by drawing two horizontal lines on a piece of paper
- Next, have someone time you to see how long it takes you to complete the next two tasks:
- On the first line, write, "I am great at multitasking"
- On the second line, write out the numbers 1-20 sequentially, like this- 1 2 3 4 5 6 7 8 9 10 11 12 13 14 15 16 17 18 19 20

Stop and check the time. How much time did it take to do the two tasks? Usually, it's about twenty seconds. Now, let's multitask:

- Draw two more horizontal lines. This time, and again have someone time you, write a letter on one line, and then a number on the line below, then the next letter in the sentence on the upper line, and then the next number in the sequence, changing from line to line. In other words, you write the letter "I" and then the number "1," then the letter "a," then the number "2," then the letter "m," then the number "3" and so on, until you complete both lines.

It is likely that once you complete this exercise, you will see that your time is double or more what it was in the first round. You also may have made some errors, and you were probably frustrated since you had to "rethink" what the next letter would be and then the following number.

You may challenge this, claiming no one operates like that. Not exactly and yet it is exactly what your brain is doing—there is no way around it.

The point is that this is switch-tasking on something incredibly simple, but it's what happens when we attempt to do two things at once. This is important because many activities that we try to multitask are far more complex than this.

Consider this: a study as far back as 2003, published in the International Journal of Information Management, found that the average person checks email once every five minutes and that it takes 64 seconds to resume the previous task after checking the email.

In other words, because of email alone, we typically waste one out of every six minutes... and that was in 2003. Imagine what those numbers look like today considering the increasingly greater dependency that we have on email. Now add to that the impact of smartphones and social media, and the problem becomes exponentially more challenging as it relates to multitasking. It is fundamentally out of control.

So, you may be wondering: if I stop multitasking, how do I reconcile all the work and information that is coming at me that's not going to slow down just because I'm exacting more self-discipline in my life?

Admittedly, there is no easy answer to this.

However, I would recommend that you begin by simply streamlining or bundling your multitasking activities. Here are some examples:

- If you like to stay informed about world news, that's great. Download one app, watch one news channel, subscribe to one news magazine. Volume is a culprit of our time evaporation. In our effort to know everything instantly, more seems to be better. Instead, we often hear the same thing over and over from different sources, just in case there is that one angle that we haven't heard. Don't do this to yourself.
- When you joined social media platforms, it made sense

to follow as many people as you could. There are many people on your feed that are distracting you more than you realize. You probably know who those people are and yet you continue to scroll past them. Take the time to reduce the number of platforms, the number of people that you follow, the number of businesses that you follow, etc. This is not about elimination- this is about moderation.

- Make a concerted effort to check your phone at the top of each hour instead of responding to every ding or vibration. I believe you will be surprised at how much multitasking activity you will eliminate. If it is impossible to resist the urge, consider taking your fingerprint unlock off and go back to the 2015 old-school-way of unlocking your phone with a passcode. After the past few years of the quick fingerprint access, you may find the passcode quite frustrating... good—it could be effective.

- If you love music like I do, designate a specific time of the day that you will listen to music, hopefully when you are relaxing and not engaged in other activities.

- When you are driving, check your phone when you get to your destination. Okay, I know you probably won't do that so check your phone only when you are stopped at a traffic light. Eliminating phone activity while you are in motion may allow you to compose the response to that text faster because you are only focused on one task. By the way, there are driving cues that you must be aware of even at a stoplight so by no means is this safe either. In the end, discipline in this space, as we have already discussed, is critical. You may save your life... and someone else's too.

- Perhaps the ultimate test. Try watching your favorite

show without using the DVR- watch it all the way through without pausing or rewinding. It may give you some insight into how distracted you are and how much multitasking has taken over your life.

- Perhaps, even go a step further. DVRS are intended to save us time- the obvious, the ability to skip commercials. The next time you are watching your favorite show, set a timer to see how long it actually took you to watch the show. You may find that the twenty-two minutes you thought that it would take to watch the latest sitcom took thirty-three minutes because of how many times you paused the DVR. By the way, when you set the timer for this activity, do not use the timer on your smartphone- you may get distracted checking social media posts. Honestly, I am not trying to be funny about this. We are lost in time with our devices and we are collectively getting less productive with time.

This entire discussion on multitasking and self-regulation is critical to this discussion of And because:

If you do not have the discipline to stop multitasking and do one thing at a time in your personal life, you may not have the ability to or even see the value in doing so in your leadership role.

The impact of multitasking in a leadership role has more profound repercussions. Consider this: have you ever had a discussion with your boss and, right in front of you, while you are talking, your boss checks his or her phone? You are right there watching. How did you feel?

That leader has done damage to your relationship and may not even know it. This person made a conscious decision that the ding on their phone could not wait. This person believed that he or she could pay attention to you while giving some attention to the phone, perhaps not realizing the obvious—you are looking at them the entire time.

Even things like the optics of "taking notes" on your phone, tablet, or laptop during a meeting can give the impression of multitasking. You may assert that this is not the situation at all—you are doing it to be more productive... until a notification banner appears on your screen and you feel compelled to check it.

You have now exited the meeting... at least for a few seconds.

Multitasking is a self-imposed behavior, and when you are leading people, they notice it every single time. This is not the same as being in a daze while engaged in a conversation. In that scenario, at least you are not demonstrating overt behaviors representing your lack of focus on the conversation.

We are at ground level here, people. This is about trying to focus on one thing at a time.

Here is one more example to demonstrate how pervasive multitasking has become. I was sitting around the boardroom table with an executive team recently—all C-level leaders.

There was a question asked of the leader of the team that was truly fascinating. Based on the context of the question, the timing of the question and the audience, it was one of the most compelling questions that I have heard anyone ask. As such, I had as much anticipation waiting for this answer as any answer I've waited for. The question was:

How do you feel about this team using our cell phones during our meeting time together?

When this question was asked, every head turned simultaneously to the leader. I mean, think about the implications of the answer to this question.

As with most things with which we have great anticipation, seconds feel like minutes: The heads turning slow-motion to look at the leader, the dramatic pause by the leader, and then finally his response. Staring across the table the leader leaned in and stated, "Look, everyone is busy so, sure, you can use them." Everyone said okay and went back to the topic at hand.

Wait, what? I could not believe the response.

This is precedent-setting stuff. This is changing the game. This is... well, present day. This is what we have become—we have acquiesced to multitasking.

Perhaps I am overreacting because I expected a different answer from that leader. Maybe I'm overreacting because of all the admonishment I've seen over the years in meetings when a participating individual "broke the code" and believed they were invisible using their cell phone in the middle of a meeting.

Listen, I am not suggesting that my recommendations on

eliminating multitasking are going to change the game—we are where we are.

However, what I am attempting to push past theory and into a place of acceptance is that multitasking and the challenges of And are self-imposed.

I am realistic, though. You may not be able to or even have a desire to stop multitasking.

First, understand that all tasks are not created equal. Hoping for efficiency by combining two simple productivity tasks like writing a letter while cleaning your kitchen counters is not realistic. There is a cognitive cost you pay of being less effective in both... with no emotional benefit.

Second, be realistic about what poor task performance might mean, given that you are not as good at multitasking as you believe. If you are not ready to eliminate secondary tasks, at least be prepared to suspend them in the moment. In the case of driving, music will always be a part of the driving experience but consider hitting mute if the conditions of driving require more focus.

You and others around you are probably going to always choose to multitask, no matter how much research is presented showing its ineffectiveness. Hopefully, you at least better understand the implications of choosing to do so. We all need to pay attention to how much or how little we are paying attention.

Let me summarize *And* this way- *And* is always more than one thing. No matter how you attempt to rationalize it *And* does not intimate one or singular.

Admittedly, all this undoing of habits takes practice. It takes practice for me. It may be unwinding bad habits, and it may require you to consciously think your way through the day. I truly believe that you will see tremendous benefits from the changes.

Let me pose one more question to the discussion of moving from And to Or and eliminating multitasking. It has nothing to do with the process or approach to the work. This is about the human element.

Let's say that you have in fact eliminated a significant amount of multitasking from your life. You even begin to see the benefits of it, but you cannot get to the productivity that you desire now because of other environmental factors.

Specifically, you are now more keenly aware of others multitasking and how it intersects your daily routines and your work and yet you cannot control the behavior of others.

So, the question then is about how to respond when others are imposing multitasking on you. Your response when this happens to you is important to this conversation about moving from And to Or. You may have to do something uncomfortable that you have been avoiding.

CHAPTER 5:

Saying No

There is another component of this journey from "And" to "Or" and that is understanding how we get ourselves into the situation in which we are forced to try to do it all. It is possible that you could be demonstrating self-discipline and focusing on one task at a time and still experience frustration due to a workload that is out of control. So, if your issue is not a lack of self-discipline or multitasking, then what is the root cause?

It could be that you have not learned how to say no. More directly, it could be that you have not learned how to say no when you *need* to say no.

This is an important distinction—saying no to the easy things is not what I am talking about. It is about saying no when it is difficult, when it is unpopular, when it feels wrong to say it.

Saying no can be very stressful, and the implications can be far-reaching and yet, saying no is perhaps the most critical element to counteract the Power Of And.

I think about the word No in this way:

No is the enemy of And.

We can spend all day talking about all the excuses and reasons why we say yes when we should say no. Rather than focus on the emotional or relational reasons for saying yes, it is time to think about the practical side of it. There are times when you cannot afford to say yes. And to be clear, a delayed yes or a maybe is not the same as No.

My point here is that we have many obstacles thrown our way almost every day, causing us to change course and make different or difficult decisions. When you do not have to be in that position, do not allow yourself to be there. I know, easy to say, but hard to do. Let's talk about how you can make it easier.

Without a doubt, there are plenty of negative connotations associated with the word No. For the sake of productivity and this conversation, there are also reasons why the word No can have positive implications, so I want to focus there.

I am not a psychologist, but some studies support the idea that saying yes is more comfortable than saying no. However, this is not about the clinical reasons. We need to understand the practical reasons why we say yes when we know that we should say no.

Understanding some of the reasons may help us find the right pivot point to begin to say no when no is the proper response. Let's look at a few potential reasons:

We Don't Want To Look Insensitive

Sometimes it is as simple as this—we don't want to look like we're insensitive to others, so we end up saying yes to every favor that is asked of us. Saying no can give the appearance that your needs are more important than the needs of others. It is especially not easy saying no to people that we care about, and sometimes they are the ones asking us most often for things that make it hard for us to say no. If those closest to you are putting you in a tough situation, you should count on the trust in your relationship to push back and ask them why they are creating this dilemma for you.

You may feel like you are insensitive by saying no, but it doesn't mean that you are. Sometimes saying yes to everything can be a big problem for everyone involved. You can empathize with others regarding their situation, but it doesn't mean that you must always do something about it.

Lack Of Confidence

Another consideration is that it can be a lack of confidence preventing you from saying no. Confidence plays a significant role in all our lives and no matter who we are and what we do, many of us may lack the confidence that we would like to have. At times, this may manifest itself in regretful yes responses. It can be difficult for many of us to stand up for ourselves.

You may have had a situation at work when your boss asked you to take on a project. You knew that you were overloaded with work already and dealing with challenges at home, but you said yes to it anyway. You may not have had enough confidence in your performance or your standing in the company to risk saying no. You may also have believed that when the next project came along, your boss wouldn't give you the opportunity.

Ultimately, a lack of confidence can lead us to agree to everything someone else asks, and we end up saying yes to things we hate because we do not have enough courage to say no.

Lastly, in any situation in which you say yes when you should say no, consider what will not get done on your list of things to do. It sounds like more tradeoffs coming... ones that you did not plan to make.

Fear Of Unacceptance

Another reason why we say yes when we should say no is perhaps the fear of unacceptance. I believe that it is human nature for us to want to feel accepted by others. At times, we fear whether we are good enough for other people. We feel obligated to say yes so that we can get the sign of approval from others.

Fear of unacceptance begins for most of us at an early age and carries over into adulthood and our work lives. Whether it is peer pressure in school with a group of friends wanting you to do something that you'd prefer not to or even deciding to engage in workplace gossip with a group of co-workers when you know that you shouldn't, it simply can be easier to comply and deal with the consequences of an affirmative response.

Finally, sometimes the easiest way to keep people in your life is by saying yes to everything. For you, the consequences of saying yes must be weighed against the value of the relationship that you are attempting to keep.

The Situation Is Uncomfortable

Sometimes we may say yes to get out of an uncomfortable situation. We may come across such a situation in life that seems impossible to avoid. We cannot think of any legitimate excuse. So, out of the frustration of not being able to justify a no response, we end up saying yes.

What you have likely done is accepted someone else's responsibility. In layman's terms, the monkey is now on your back and off their back.

In general, overcommitting to responsibilities by saying yes to everything can be problematic for everyone. Not only are you frustrated, but the quality of your output may also suffer because you are rushing it and the person that created the situation to make you feel forced, is likely not happy with the final product either. It is a lose-lose situation.

For those of you that are parents, think about how many times you may have cleaned up your child's room. I am confident that there were times when you gave them directions to clean their room, and they didn't do so. You were then faced with a dilemma. Repeat the order, discipline them, or do it yourself. Inherently, only you know the right answer in your situation. However, I suspect this situation many times was 'resolved' when you cleaned the room yourself. It's okay, it is almost a rite of passage for being a parent.

The issue here is that you didn't say no—you said yes and took time away from something else that you could have been doing... even if it was to relax, especially if it was to relax. You justify it in your mind that it is only ten minutes of your time to clean up the room, you can clean it up faster than your child can, you know everything will get put where it goes and what you were going to do was not that important anyway... and, and, and – the psyche of being a parent.

It's a funny example, but is it really that funny?

If you cannot say no to a five-year-old, you must think about what chance you have of saying no to your boss or someone else at work heaping an unrealistic amount of work on your plate.

Saying No is a difficult concept for many of us in our daily lives, and it starts in our personal lives. I believe that you must begin by saying no in your personal life when a no response is needed.

Let's face it, we find ourselves having trouble saying no when we pass by the store in the neighborhood where Girl Scouts are selling cookies or saying no to the salesman coming to our front door (although we see a lot less of that now than in prior generations), or saying no when offered a credit card or loyalty program in a store.

In fact, in many parts of our daily lives, businesses are preying on us and counting on us to say yes. That may seem a bit exaggerated, but I would submit that marketers and consultants are sitting around boardroom tables, hedging tactics and promotions designed to get a yes acceptance rate that can justify the initiative.

I would also submit that many of you have something in your closet or garage that you bought as a result of saying yes when you know that you should have said no. Exhibit A- I still have a Kirby vacuum sitting in my garage that I bought twenty years ago from a door-to-door salesman whom I allowed to come in and make his pitch. There is a bit of saving grace—at least the vacuum still works.

So yes, being able to say no in your personal life is an excellent place to start — a place to practice it and perfect it. I am not a self-help guru recommending that you stand in front of the mirror and say no one hundred times each morning before getting your day started. Instead, say it just once when it matters, when you are faced with an important yes or no decision.

When you are faced with critical yes or no situations, and there are plenty of them throughout every day. I am recommending a couple of things:

- Ask yourself, what is the worst thing that can happen if I say no? I get it, there will be situations where the consequence of saying no is too great, so do not say no in those situations. However, the answer cannot always be yes.
- Ask yourself, have I always said yes to this request before? If so, how different will the dynamics be if I say no this time?

Saying No can be the most liberating experience that you can have in your personal or professional life. It can keep you away from the pitfalls of just saying yes and then attempting to manage the situation.

As a leader, you have a different responsibility because the implications of saying yes or no are different. It doesn't mean that you arbitrarily need to begin to say no more often as a result of your role, but the lens through which you make decisions may need to change and that may ultimately prompt you to say no more often.

In my recent COO (chief operating officer) role, I was faced with a full-scale business turnaround. Every day was filled with new challenges, maybe better described as surprises, and plenty of tough decisions that needed to be made.

Because there were so many moving parts and so many things that needed to be fixed all at once, saying no felt impossible. So, most days, I didn't say no.

Let me provide some context to this. Before taking the COO role, I had already worked thirty-three years of retail; I had experienced working in high-pressure situations, working for founder-led businesses, working directly with founders, working with franchisees and licensees, working with consultants and even with organizations going out of business. I would say that I had seen a lot and had been in positions in which I had to say no and did say no.

In the COO role though, most days I said yes and worked

tirelessly to figure it all out. I realized throughout the time in this role that my default response had become yes. As a result, I also realized that my default response in my personal life was also yes—a different challenge for me to solve and one that I attempted to decouple from the work situation. Given that I am the same person at work or at home, that didn't work out so well.

What I found was that the personal inability to say no to family members, friends, and others was adding pressure to the work situation, if for no other reason than it was compressing my time. I felt an obligation to say yes because these were people that were close to me. At the same time, I felt just as much responsibility to say yes to the people with whom I worked.

So back to the COO role and why this is so critical. Like the discussion about self-discipline and how the implications are different personally versus professionally, not being able to say no has the potential to exhibit the same type of impact.

What I failed to realize for my first year or so in the COO role was that I was creating stress on my team as many of them were doing the work that was a result of my affirmative responses. This was not my intention, but a valuable lesson learned. As a leader, what you sign up for is also what your team signs up for... they just don't know it. Also, the larger the scale of your role, it is likely that an automatic yes response creates even more work.

I can remember a specific turning point, though. Almost one year to the day into the role, I was inundated with work, truly feeling the pressure. It felt like the more work that we completed, the longer became the list of things to do. What I realized was that so much of my time was being spent on work that was unrelated to my role and, therefore, unrelated to the functions of those on my team.

I had to admit and own the fact that I had placed myself in a situation in which I was taking on work from too many other people in the organization. It was often disguised as operational work, so I took it. As a result, I was unintentionally heaping this work on my team as well. Perhaps I felt guilty because other departments seemed to have an even heavier workload than the operations team or the field team did, if that was even possible.

As often occurs, when you do a post-mortem on a situation, you get to the ground truth. Mine was this: I didn't have the courage to say no.

So, on this day, after one year into the role, I recall being asked to make a trip to spend with a franchisee and their group of field leaders. The work described for the project was entirely out of the scope of my role and my department's role... and I knew it right away.

For the first time, I could see it clearly, and I knew what I had to do. I suppose I should not be so hard on myself since I was still learning the organization and the people just one year into the role. After all, I'm not sure that I could have recognized this gap in the first year of a new position. At least, these are the excuses that I told myself.

I remember saying no that day and with such conviction that

I immediately felt liberated. Not only did I not take on the assignment, but I also declined to allow any of my team to participate in it as well. I knew how valuable their time was and that they were feeling the same workload pressure that I'd been feeling. I felt like giving the team a high five and letting them know of what I just saved them from, and then I realized that was just my job, my responsibility.

You don't get credit for "saves" in leadership~you have the responsibility to simply do the right thing.

It was a complete game-changer, though. It changed the course of the role for my team and me, it changed the way others approached me with work, and I found myself not needing to say no as often any longer simply because of one no response that changed the behavior of others around me.

Now, you may say that responding to a situation with a 'no' one time in your life doesn't usually create that level of change. I would say that it depends, and you can't possibly know until you say no for the first time.

If the analogy of getting the monkey off my back fits for this situation, then I had a 900-pound gorilla extracted. It truly was getting this very clingy, gripping problem off my back that wasn't going to go away until I did something different-and that something different was saying no. I also learned that, even when others see the monkey on your back, they are not always inclined to help you get it off, only because it could mean that they have to put it on their own backs. Interesting how this all works.

Think of it this way: saying no may stop just as much additional work as the amount of extra work that is created when you continue to say yes. Said differently, there could be a double benefit to productivity by saying no.

So, No is the enemy of And. And is saying I will do this and that, and that sounds like two yes responses to me.

And is a powerful word. It means more; it means yes, it means this and that, it means a lot.

No invites Or into the conversation. Inviting Or into the conversation, almost by definition means you will say yes to some things and no to other things—balance.

This gets back to the fundamental concept of the Power of Or.

The Power Of Or is about the delicate balance of having a clarity of purpose on what is important, what is not important, the ability to distinguish between the two, and then taking the appropriate action on those priorities to achieve the desired results — Choosing and Doing What Matters Most.

The Power of Or is that you cannot do it all. The Power Of Or is that you should not want to do it all.

You must say no to something, maybe a lot of things.

To say no becomes a process of weighing your choices... and choices are plentiful.

CHAPTER 6:

A Choice Is A Choice

Let's look at the basics. What is a choice exactly?

In the purest form, a choice is our ability to make decisions when presented with two or more options.

Most choices are not life or death. Many of us may never make a life or death choice, though there are decisions that just feel like it. In those situations, it is likely that we have other underlying factors to address.

Choice can be difficult because it can represent sacrifice. Choosing something means giving up something else—something we might want later, but that likely won't be available to us if we do not get it right now. That feeling can leave you with regrets about the choices you have made.

We live in an unprecedented age of options... and that level of choice can make decisions even more difficult. I often think about the simplicity of life when I was a teenager compared to the options, and ultimately, the choices, that were available to my children as teenagers and even now to the next generation.

Simple things like going from five television channels in 1980 to hundreds, even thousands of channels today. Before any of the technological advances of the past forty years or so, it was simple. You turned on the television and watched the few shows available to you, and once they were finished, you never saw them again—no reruns.

I am certainly not saying that simple was better, but I'm sure that we were left with far more brain cells at the end of the day. There were parts of our lives where choices didn't exist as they do today.

It can feel like the overwhelming number of choices now available potentially outweighs the number of decisions that we need to make and the time that is even available to make them.

How about this headline: according to a recent study by the research firm Dscout, we touch our smartphones around 2,617 times... daily! I know, I had the same reaction when I first heard this—surely it cannot be physically possible to touch your phone that many times in a day.

For the study, Dscout recruited a demographically diverse sample of ninety-four smartphone users from a pool of more than 100,000 participants across the U.S.

Then they built a supplementary smartphone tool to track every user's interaction across five days, twenty-four hours a day.

Researchers found that based on the total amount of swipes, clicks, likes, and posts, the total amount of touches was on average a whopping 2,617 times each day. For the heaviest users—the top ten percent—average interactions more than doubled to 5,427 touches a day.

This was time that included activities like typing texts, swiping on pictures, turning Kindle pages, and scrolling on Facebook.

According to a networkworld.com article, the average smartphone user engages in seventy-six separate phone sessions a day. Heavy users, the top ten percent, averages 132 sessions a day.

I understand, the numbers seem impossible. Perhaps, no more impossible than the facts which show that we touch our face hundreds of times a day... and we are not even aware of it.

Need more data? Another recent study says that we now check or unlock our phones more than eighty times a day. Millennials and Generation Z alone unlock their phones 150 times a day, and some users are reported to unlock their phones more than 300 times a day. No matter how simple the interactions, every browse of the phone is a choice, even to what we decide to read or not to read. With what we do read, it usually requires some additional choices or decision-making.

I must admit that I was astonished by these unlock numbers as well. I didn't believe it, so I did my own test. I kept track for a week of how many times I unlocked my phone. I thought that being aware of it might change my behavior; perhaps I would do it less. The reality is that I am just as attached to technology as the next person. I averaged sixty-seven unlock sessions per day! While many of my unlocks were related to work and checking emails, the result was still shocking to me.

Inside of each session of unlocking the phone, I also found my behavior very similar to the Dscout test, as my total touches were around two thousand per day!

To be clear, this is not a lecture about using our smartphones too much; I would sound like my parents if I said that. What I am saying is that a choice is a choice, a choice is an activity or action, and choice takes time. No matter how quick you are on the trigger with your phone, after a couple hundred or couple thousand choices throughout a day, you will expend a lot of mental energy—mental power that you will wish you had later in the day.

Aside from social media, we are confronted with a barrage of choices every day. We make choices about what we wear, what we eat, the places that we decide to go, the people we meet, and so on.

Of course, one of the natural paths to reducing choices is to simply reduce the number of decisions you need to make so that you can focus on something else. Giving up choice is not easy, though.

I think about my own decision years ago when it was time to select a financial advisor.

The person that I ultimately chose, came recommended to me,

basically gift-wrapped. He was recommended by a former boss whom I completely trusted and whose money he was already managing. With all of that, and the fact that my former boss had far more assets than I did, I still sat on the decision for over two years! This was not because of how much the financial advisor services would cost, or even as a matter of trust, but mostly because someone else would be making choices with my money that I am accustomed to making and of course, I felt more equipped to make. With all the decisions that I had to make at that time in my life, and with so many choices, I still didn't want to give up any decision-making authority. That is how difficult giving up choice can be.

So, to say just get rid of some of your choices to make decision-making more manageable is not so simple.

While having an abundance of choices might sound appealing, studies have found that it often causes us to feel stressed and overwhelmed.

In a world where speed matters more, choice is complicating the matter. The notion that choice is always good for people–the more choices, the better seems intuitively wrong.

In the early days of social media, I remember making an active choice when I added myself to a new platform, I took myself off another one, to manage my number of things to check daily. That worked for me. To invest the time to be proficient in a new social media platform, I needed to let go of a different one.

In a matter of years, the world changed a lot, and I felt compelled to stay aware of what was happening. So, I got back on all the social media platforms that I had abandoned, and I began clicking and swiping more than ever before. Right or wrong, I equated choice with knowledge. I have only recently had an awakening and took my own advice and abandoned all the social media platforms except for one. By the way, I feel better already about giving up those choices.

With so much choice available, it becomes a question of how to ensure that you are making the right choices. I'm not sure that there is a clear-cut answer to this, but good choices are likely ones that align with the direction in which you want to go and that you feel good about long after you've made a decision.

Wrong choices can end up being counterproductive, can spike your stress levels and leave you hesitant to make decisions in the future.

I know that you are probably looking for more depth in that answer, but let's continue to discuss choice as it may reveal more of what you're looking for related to what constitutes a good choice.

I recently went and studied choice and decision-making by observing people at a mall on a typical Thursday and then engaged some of them in conversation about their shopping behavior.

A mall is an interesting environment in which to watch people. One, because it is a captive environment with a vast cross-section of people. Mostly though, for this exercise, the mall is interesting because of the number of choices and decisions that are continually being made, consciously or subconsciously.

That said, I was not sure what I was going to observe. I could not remember the last time that I had spent time in a mall, and I am confident that whenever the last time was, it was not my decision to be there.

I know that my change in behavior is not all that uncommon. Let's face it. Malls are not what they used to be. All the financial indicators have pointed to the decline in mall traffic for years and year on year. A whole host of contributing factors have surfaced: online shopping, the demand for convenience, and the rise of free-standing discount retailers, to name a few. Malls still have their moments though, like Black Friday weekend.

Nonetheless, here I was headed to the now mostly novelty concept called a mall. Again, this was a typical Thursday, and I suppose that what I saw was typical. It was odd, though, to see so many empty parking lots as I circled the mall. Many of the large anchor tenants were either out of business or looked like they were out of business. Parking lots that boasted the ability to hold 400-500 cars in front of an anchor store twenty years ago were now an oversized sidewalk leading up to the mall.

Once inside the mall, I was surprised to see the number of businesses that were boarded up. Maybe that is too dramatic— out of business is more appropriate. I saw a lot of the usual suspects in terms of brands still doing business in the mall— brands that I remember being there twenty years ago. Perhaps that is part of the problem, same old brands and no compelling reason for many newer, trendier brands to move in.

There was a decent number of people walking around, though, likely because it was still summer.

I believe that being absent from the mall for years prior to this visit worked to my advantage as I had fewer preconceived notions about what I would see. I just didn't know.

What I did know was that every storefront a customer passed by represented a decision being made, active or passive, on whether to stop and if so, for how long, what to look at, what to purchase, how to pay, etc., so I felt confident that I would be able to capture key insights about choices and decision-making.

So, I watched. I was in the mall for a total of ten hours. I observed customer behavior in two-hour blocks from 11:00 a.m.- 1:00 p.m., not long after the mall opened. I believe that seeing the decisions that customers make at the beginning of the day was an important data point to capture.

I also observed customers from 3:00 p.m.-5:00 p.m. I believed this to be a different mix of customers and in the middle of the day for most people and therefore, more of a midpoint of all the decisions that they would make for the day.

The third observation period was 7:00 p.m.-9:00 p.m. Of course, that ran up to closing time for the mall, and this, I believed, was a third separate customer cohort in demographics and purpose. These were also customers that had either come from work or school and had likely made considerably more decisions throughout the day compared to those customers that I had tracked earlier in the day.

I gave myself a two-hour gap between each observation to synthesize what I had observed and of course, to rest and ensure that I was as attentive for each observation session as I was for the others. So, here is what I learned:

The key learning straightaway from this process: customers in the morning, in the afternoon and in the evening, all basically behaved the same. Admittedly, I did have one preconceived notion going into this—that people would behave differently by time of day. In the end, the similarity in behavior was more helpful as it expanded my sample size into one large group.

Another key learning—while there were many key messages at each storefront related to sales and offers, the customers seemed to be oblivious to those messages and did not appear to make any choices because of the messages—so much wasted money spent on signs.

Eighty-five percent of the customers seemed to have a store or a couple of stores in mind as their reason for coming to the mall. That was clear in the body language, as more than seventy percent of the customers throughout the day didn't break stride until they reached the store that was on their list to visit. It was also confirmed as I questioned customers that I tracked throughout the day.

For those that did stop in front of a store, fifteen percent of the customers, the average person spent twenty-three seconds at the storefront before deciding to go in—much longer than I would have expected. However, the decision to go in or continue walking to the next store was unaffected by a store employee. Thirty percent of the time, there was a store employee that engaged the customer at the front of the store. However, the percentage of customers the employee engaged with that went in the store was no different than stores where the customer peeking in had no engagement from an employee.

When I spoke to mall patrons, one of the questions I asked was whether they would frequent the mall if they had a choice to go somewhere else—a choice question about choice. The majority (seventy-five percent) said that if the store(s) they wanted to visit had a location outside of the mall, they would not come to the mall. As I dug further, they had precise reasons. They cited parking at the mall as a deterrent for coming more often- it is difficult to park near the store(s) where they want to shop. A bit of an oddity as there were large, unoccupied parking lots outside. However, many of the customers stated that they were not coming to shop at an anchor store- in fact, a little more than fifty percent. For those entering the mall at a traditional mall opening, this meant a longer walk to get to their destination.

When questioned about the stores that they were drawn to in the mall, many customers stated that they were coming to shop at stores that still have very little online presence or that offered in-store items or promotions that were not available online. That seemed counterintuitive to the way that commerce is being driven now, but the mall appeared to still have some appeal, albeit far less than in previous years.

I also asked the customers why they liked coming to the mall. An interesting response that came up from a small portion of the mall shoppers was that the mall was not destination shopping. They could go and perhaps find something that they didn't know they wanted. The variety of passing more than a hundred stores was enticing to them—more choices. That was only about twenty-five percent, though.

I asked a question about what influenced what they purchased. The top three responses were:

- It was affordable
- It was something that they needed
- It was something that they could carry

And in that order. The only dynamic that changed for some with this question was for those who tried on clothes. Of course, how they looked in clothing surged to the top of the responses for those customers.

Some other data points. Customers, on average:

- spent one hour and thirty-seven minutes in the mall
- Spent $87 total in an average of three stores—this included food purchases
- Eighty-three percent used credit cards, and seventeen percent used cash for tender

I asked one final question of each customer that I intercepted on that day: How do you feel? I intentionally asked it without any additional context to gauge how customers perceived the question.

Almost to a person, and without any prompting from me, an overwhelming majority of the customers said, "tired." Interesting... so I probed.

More than sixty percent of the mall customers on that day said that they were mentally tired, versus only forty percent that said they were physically exhausted. So, I probed even more. In general, the sixty percent mentally tired cited too many stores, too many things to look at, too many options. Of course, the forty percent stating physical exhaustion was what you would expect, the number of steps needed to shop in the mall.

I left with a solid understanding of the customer behavior in the mall and the taxing impact of choice. Overall, I would summarize it this way—the mall is a combination of many stores to choose from, many items to choose from in each store, a high level of messaging in each store, and an environment that combines so many of our needs in one place—clothing, food, entertainment and other needs. It is choice overload.

One final takeaway. Shopping at a mall is an interesting dynamic as it can equally zap both physical and mental energy at the same time.

With choice, there are so many dimensions—many more than just volume.

Even when we choose well, we are often less satisfied because, with so many choices, we are seduced into believing that somewhere out there is something better.

One of three things is likely to occur when people have too many choices. We end up making poor decisions, we are more dissatisfied with our choices, or we become paralyzed and do not choose at all.

More and more choice does not guarantee better options, just more of them. You are debilitating yourself by making inconsequential decisions all day long, mostly due to the volume of choices.

Some of the challenges of choice-making arise with options that may feel right in the short-term but may incrementally take you off course over the longer term. For example, having that one extra cookie or drinking that one additional beer is an example of this.

Conversely, some choices can be a bit painful at the time but lead to better results down the road. For example, staying home and studying instead of going to the big party or forcing yourself to go to the gym after a long day of work are examples of short-term discomfort that pays off later.

I recently conducted another experiment related to choices.

I decided to download food delivery apps... all of them. Of course, knowing what I know now, I would have been better served to select a couple of them. Nonetheless, downloading all of them works much better for the point being made in this book. I downloaded everything available in my area- many of the usual suspects that you may use.

For twenty-one days, I used each service, at least five orders on each app to ensure that I would have enough comparison data.

The delivery service has become a very crowded space. I wasn't sure what I was going to learn, but I can tell you that I learned a lot. So much of what I learned had to do with even more choices than I had envisioned.

First, the process to modify items, the process to add items to the cart and the process to checkout were all relatively straightforward, intuitive, and similar. The navigation of each app overall, in general was intuitive as well. There were some nuances like:

On one app, there was a small delivery fee of $2.00 for orders under $8.00- so a chocolate shake all in totaled $11.20. Unbelievable! I only ordered that one time.

On another app, there are "pass programs" for $9.99 a month- delivery fees are waived on orders over $15. But like any other pass or subscription type program, use it often, or it is not financially worth it. Of course, the company is counting on you not using it regularly. I know, a bit cynical.

Also, the actual delivery itself was a differentiator. Two of the services used their employees to deliver, and it mattered. I thought that perhaps I had a bias at first, giving credit to the fact that the app and the actual delivery were branded and bundled together. It felt like more care. It was more care. The order came faster, and the quality of the order was better—not just the first time, but every time.

The most significant lesson learned is that the options are even more overwhelming than I had imagined.

One app had 248 restaurants listed. I had no idea that so many restaurants were in the entire city, let alone in the range of delivering to me.

One app had a "$3 or less" category- I didn't know that it was even possible to find anything for three dollars, but I greatly appreciated the value play. I was really excited until I clicked and realized, it was a three dollar or less delivery charge. Oh, that made more sense. That app also had eighteen categories, defined by types of foods, like Mexican, Italian, etc.- overwhelming. Maybe I was expecting too much or perhaps too little.

A third app had categories like "Under twenty-five minutes" and "free delivery," but overall, fifty-four categories!

I can say that I was mentally exhausted after going through the process. I spent an average of nine minutes deciding what to order and placing the order, over twenty-five percent of the time that it took to get my food, added to the delivery time of twenty-six minutes on average. I must admit, there were moments of— get in the car and go get it. It will be faster and easier.

The first time on each app was long—an average of twelve minutes. To be fair, the primary interaction required account information, setting a password, etc., and then placing an order, so no doubt that was exhausting. However, the subsequent app uses, because I intentionally did not reorder the same items, were still lengthy due to modifications and just general searching for items.

I walked away from the delivery experience with greater understanding, but with less desire than I thought that I would have to use delivery again in the future. That said, I can envision select meal occasions with delivery being a necessary evil. Perhaps evil is the operative word here.

Delivery is just one example of how our lives are changing every day.

So much choice can be exhausting though. I am often banned from choosing a movie at home from any of the streaming services. My instinct is to take control and, being the movie connoisseur that I am, find that gem of a movie that would impress everyone. I mean, after all, I did work at Blockbuster for fourteen years and watched thousands of movies. So, the problem is that I worked for Blockbuster for fourteen years and watched thousands of videos—everything looks good to me.

I will digress for a moment. I often reminisce about the days when people would walk the New Release wall at Blockbuster. It was not uncommon to spend thirty minutes walking and reading movie synopses before making a selection. That was an enjoyable activity for many people. After all, this mostly occurred on the weekend, and it was a way of rewarding yourself for making it through the week. And oh, you didn't have so many other decisions to make throughout your week like social media clicks and ten thousand television channels. Wow, those were great times.

So, back to the streaming services. After 175 scrolls, reading forty-five movie synopses, and fourteen minutes later, I had not selected a movie and, when I finally found a worthy movie, everyone else had moved on to something else. And, in this process, I had used more brain cells than I used on a final exam.

Choice is the purest expression of free will. The freedom to choose allows us to shape our lives exactly as we wish.

In the end, the volume of choices may be detrimental to our making quality decisions, leading to the conclusion that one of the keys to answering the question about making right choices may simply be to have fewer of them.

The amount of choice may not be an inhibitor to good decisions for everyone, but it may create fatigue that impacts the decisions that we make.

CHAPTER 7:

Decision Fatigue

When you expend so much energy on choices throughout the day, you are left with what is called **decision fatigue**.

There have been hundreds of articles written about decision fatigue in just the last decade, simply because this problem has grown exponentially in recent years due to the proliferation of choices.

When we are fresh and most alert, we make the best decisions we can with the information that is available. However, as we increase the number of decisions that we make throughout the day, we begin to lose the ability to make good ones. Enter decision fatigue.

The best way that I can define decision fatigue is: Decision fatigue is a form of mental fatigue.

We have always understood physical fatigue. If you run a twenty-six-mile marathon, unless you are a robot, it is universally accepted that you will be more fatigued physically at the end of the marathon than you were at the beginning. For some reason, we have not always applied the same principle to mental fatigue.

However, decision fatigue can be deceptive—it is not like physical fatigue. You probably do not feel tired at the end of the day, and yet your decisions become more irrational.

Mental fatigue has been associated with things like lack of rest and high levels of stress. Of course, stress can cause many things. However, decision fatigue can occur even after a good night of sleep and even with a manageable level of stress in your life because it is about the volume of choices with which you are faced throughout the day. Decision fatigue is not always noticeable and therein lies the problem. For example:

Think about when you have gone to look for an apartment. The energy and excitement that you have when the day begins looks very different by the end of the day when you have already looked at seven apartments and they all begin to look the same. You have moved from wanting to find the perfect apartment to a level of frustration in which any apartment will do. That is decision fatigue.

Making decisions takes effort and the more difficult decisions cause us to expend even more energy. As we become tired, we are less able to accurately weigh all the factors involved in making a good decision. As a result, we make more subconscious decisions as our self-control is waning. Decision fatigue is a huge factor in overall mental fatigue, and decision fatigue is just as taxing on your brain as physical fatigue is on your body.

To fully understand decision fatigue, it is essential to understand the complexity of the human brain. There is a scientific aspect of this that is worth exploring so allow me to geek out for a moment and delve into the complexity of the human brain.

Consider this: Back in 2014, a team from Japan and Germany carried out a record simulation of the human brain, in the largest neuronal network simulation to date—and yet achieved a model of only one second of human brain activity. That required forty minutes for the computer to do so. The joint project was carried out by the Japanese research group RIKEN, the Okinawa Institute of Science, Technology Graduate University and Forschungszentrum Jülich, a German based research center.

The team used RIKEN's K computer, which has its home in Kobe, Japan, known for exceptional precision and computational power and ranked as one of the world's most-powerful supercomputers, to simulate human brain activity.

The team made use of the open-source Neural Simulation Technology (NEST) tool. The NEST project site describes it as a simulator ideal for networks spiking neurons of any size. NEST was put to work to replicate a network of 1.73 billion nerve cells and 10.4 trillion synapses.

All that activity by an incredible supercomputer over a forty minute span and all that it could do was simulate one second of human brain activity. That demonstrates the complexity of the human brain.

That was then...

More recently, the next generation of computers, called Exascale, are computers which can carry out a quintillion floating-point operations per second, which is an important milestone in computing, as it is thought to be the same power as a human brain and therefore opens the door to the potential real-time simulation of the human brain's activity.

The newly formed million-processor-core 'Spiking Neural Network Architecture' or 'SpiNNaker' machine can complete more than two hundred million, million actions per second, with each of its chips having one hundred million moving parts.

Developed by the Advanced Processor Technologies Research Group at the School of Computer Science, University of Manchester, the SpiNNaker machine can model more biological neurons in real-time than any other device on the planet.

SpiNNaker is unique because, unlike traditional computers, it doesn't communicate by sending large amounts of information from point A to B via a standard network. Instead, it mimics the massively parallel communication architecture of the brain, sending billions of small amounts of information simultaneously to thousands of different destinations.

The ultimate objective for the project has always been a million cores in a single computer for real-time brain modeling applications.

The computer's creators eventually aim to model up to a billion biological neurons in real-time and are now a step closer. To give an idea of scale, a mouse brain consists of around 100 million neurons, and the human brain is 1000 times bigger than that.

One billion neurons are one percent of the scale of the human brain, which consists of just under 100 billion brain cells, or neurons, which are all highly interconnected via approximately one quadrillion-that is one with fifteen zeros- synapses.

So, what is the point here? If the greatest computers in the world are having a difficult time keeping up with the human brain, it underscores the complexities and the amazing abilities that we possess inside of our head.

Why this is important is that we are using our brain, with all its possibilities, to make trivial choices. Ultimately, we are weaving in and out of choices all day long that have very little meaning when our brains could be spending time saving the world... literally.

Now back to more of the practical aspect of decision fatigue. I have personally seen decision fatigue play out by reflecting on all the years I worked at Starbucks. As far back as 2009 at Starbucks, we proudly touted the fact that we had more than 87,000 drink combinations. By the time I left the organization, it was well over 100,000 drink combinations.

I think about the decision fatigue of being a barista at Starbucks. There are no drink recipe cards posted in the stores, so yes, your barista is making your special drink from memory—that is incredible, and it is incredibly exhausting. Just consider how many brain cells that recall activity is consuming every day… and that is before the baristas begin to make decisions for the rest of their day.

Decision fatigue is not a one-time event. It is about the cumulative effect and hundreds of beverages made every shift is a cumulative effect.

This is relevant because this activity is not the same impact on your brain as, let's say, watching a movie. When you are watching a movie, your brain gets a rest from whatever it has been working on—even if it is only for a few hours. A movie allows your brain to unplug and re-energize. Your mind is focused on the present moment and it lets go of all other concerns in your life- of course, this is only true if you are paying attention to the movie.

Think of the impact on the brain of watching a movie as a car idling in park. The engine is still on but using the least amount of power. Now back to the Starbucks example and the impact of recalling beverage recipes. This is just the opposite. In the example of the car, this is more like sitting in the car in park and pushing on the gas to rev the engine. Decision fatigue is like that.

There are plenty of millennials and Generation Z working at Starbucks right now experiencing decision fatigue due to the amount of memory capacity and recall needed to make drinks, losing brain cells that they will never get back. Again, little decisions, but a cumulative effect of deciding in what order to make those drinks, how much room to leave at the top of an Americano and choosing the right pump, scoop, shake, etc... all shift long.

Of course, it is not all gloom-and-doom. The feeling of someone taking time to remember what you like to drink is a powerful point of connection, and one of the most compelling aspects of differentiation at Starbucks and others in retail that have cult-like followings.

Again, I don't want to get too far into academia with my approach, but I have a friend who is a therapist that has found himself becoming a "millennial or Generation Z therapist"— clearly a term that is a sign of the times. I will digress for a moment.

There is a lot to be said about Millennials, and there has been a lot said about them. I believe that they are a very smart, knowledgeable, and ambitious cohort that bridges the gap between old thinking and new thinking.

I am fully aware that I am about to make a broad, general statement: Millennials are empathetic, they care about social concerns that I never considered at their age, and diversity and inclusion is not an option with them. They accept others. To that extent, Millennials demonstrate behaviors that I envy.

All these things could be said about Generation Z as well, based on how they stand up for issues that they believe in... at an even earlier age.

All that said, I believe that there are anxieties that can hold Millennials back and potentially Generation Z to an even higher degree.

What I have heard from my children—a Millennial and two from Generation Z, are things like: "I am worried that I am not already successful," "I feel like a failure," and the classic "I don't want to adult today." What I see the most, though, is the struggle with making decisions, mostly due to having an unreasonable number of choices—for almost everything.

So, back to choices and decision fatigue.

Decision fatigue is a factor, especially in today's world, where we are overloaded with information and have more pressure than ever to succeed. There are so many big life decisions to make: what college to attend, what career to choose, what car to drive, where to live, how to manage our money, and so much more.

When Former President Barack Obama was in office, he was often described as being a boring dresser- he never wore anything flashy or even hinted at the temptation to stray from the bland, basic colors. There was a reason for it.

The Former President Obama, on why he only wears grey or blue suits- he says, "I am trying to pare down decisions. I don't want to make decisions about what I am eating or wearing, because I have too many other decisions to make."

Former President Obama isn't the only leader who does this. Facebook co-founder and CEO, Mark Zuckerberg, wears the same outfits every day as well. This was also true of the late Apple co-founder and CEO Steve Jobs. You can see a pattern here among some very successful people.

I can appreciate their discipline to limit their choices in decision-making. Even with this level of discipline, it still doesn't get you to the finish line. There are still more choices that each of them must consider—things called accessories... belt, watch, tie-color, shoes, cufflinks. Women have their own set of outfit and accessory choices to consider, as well.

This demonstrates just how many choices that we must make every day... even when we attempt to simplify them.

In this example, it is not that these three men have a poor fashion sense. It is that they understand that too many choices cause decision fatigue.

Eliminating repetitive decision-making is one way to reduce decision fatigue—decisions like scrolling on social media. These may all feel like inconsequential decisions. Perhaps they are, but there are now hundreds of decisions like these every day that did not exist years ago.

As you make more decisions throughout the day, your reserve of judgment and willpower can become depleted. As you become more mentally fatigued, you will start to make decisions impulsively instead of carefully thinking through consequences.

Decision fatigue helps explain why ordinarily sensible people eat well throughout the day but succumb to a poor dinner choice or some late-night junk food, even though they know better.

Once your mental energy is depleted, you become susceptible to making tradeoffs, which is an entirely different dimension of decision-making. Tradeoffs lead to compromise, and compromise leads to a reduced level of willpower. Ultimately, decision fatigue leaves you vulnerable to making poor choices.

In short: The more choices and decisions, simple or complex, you are subjected to, the less mental energy and willpower you have left at the end of the day.

I recognize that I am beating a steady drum on this subject of decision fatigue: it is that important.

So, there have always been choices. There is no getting around it. Problems can arise when there are too many choices.

Most of this discussion about decision fatigue has been focused on how it impacts us personally, but there are also implications for leadership. When it comes to leadership and making decisions in an organization, you must also consider decision fatigue.

Whether your challenge with decision fatigue is personal or professional, there are a few things that I would recommend:

Become A Decision-Making Minimalist

Do like the three previously mentioned leaders and be a minimalist on the things that don't matter, like what to wear. Life can be lived more fully when small and unnecessary decisions are made for you. Minimalism leaves you more room to focus on more important decisions.

For example, when you are selecting movies on a streaming service, take advantage of the queue option. The first time that you decide to invest thirty minutes in looking for a movie to watch, click on everything that is of interest to you and add it to your queue. What you have effectively done is eliminated hundreds, maybe even thousands of choices that you will not have to scroll through the next time.

While a lot of people choose to apply minimalism to what they wear or what they eat, it can be applied to any part of your life.

Make The Most Important Decisions Early

Next, make your most critical and strategic decisions in the morning... just in case. You may still feel mentally alert to make decisions at the end of the day, but it is likely that you are not as mentally alert as you were to begin the day. Think about the marathon runner. The point here is don't leave to chance making the most important decisions when you are likely not at your best.

Your mind is the clearest during the morning hours because you have not worn yourself down from so many activities, choices and decisions. You are still more inclined in the morning to stop and think about your choices more carefully.

Even for those that do not profess to being "morning persons," this is not about when you wake up, this is about making important decisions whenever your day begins.

Choose Simpler Options When Available

For the lower priority things on your list that really have no significance, go for the simpler option or better yet, just skip it altogether. If you must do it, do it simply and quickly.

One challenge in decision-making is treating easy decisions as if they were difficult and important in the long run. Back to my peanut butter example, I stood in the store and contemplated the pros and cons of the different varieties for far too long. This was a waste of time, yet it is a very common experience.

Eat To Mitigate Decision Fatigue

Makes sense—many of us are irritable if we have not eaten when our body is craving food, so making important decisions when we are cranky cannot be good either. But this goes deeper than that.

We have all heard that it is not a good idea to go grocery shopping when you are hungry, but research suggests that we should not make any important decisions on an empty stomach.

There is a hormone called ghrelin that your stomach produces, which negatively impacts decision making. This hormone decreases impulse control and increases your appetite. This bad combination works to increase your chance of making a bad decision. Because of this, it is important to make sure that you have had enough to eat before making any big decision, especially later in the day.

Examine whether you are making decisions that you need to make or whether you have taken on the decision-making responsibilities of others around you. Again, part of the unlock here is to not inundate yourself with so many choices and decisions that you deplete your mental energy early in the day.

Delegation is not a core competency in most companies and yet it is one element that stymies the effectiveness of so many leaders.

One of the challenges with decision fatigue is that most of us often don't realize it when it is happening. Very much like the discussion about multitasking—if you have made it a practice to sift through thousands of choices every day to make many decisions that you should not have to make, this may be your new normal. You may not actually detect the amount of decision fatigue that you are experiencing.

So, when it comes to choices, more is not necessarily better. More can leave you feeling frustrated. Ultimately, I believe that reducing your choices can, not only help you make better decisions, but also enable you to make them quicker.

In fact, getting down to two options when you must make a

decision might be the optimal situation to accelerate decision-making and minimize decision fatigue. Surely A or B seems more manageable than A or B or C or D or E.

CHAPTER 8:

This Or That

A choice is simply an act of making a decision when faced with two or more possibilities.

Fundamentally, it is choosing this or that, or in the case of more than two possibilities, choosing this or that or that—you get the point. This chapter is focused on whittling your choices down to two options and then deciding.

You may be thinking, well, why not just get to the final decision? I believe there are many simple decisions that we make quickly every day, either because we have made the same decision before as part of our daily routine or we've got choices that are agreeable to our belief system, therefore making the decision easy to make.

However, for the more difficult decisions, particularly ones with many choices to consider and ones we make in a leadership role that can have financial or human implications on the organization, narrowing to two options can be beneficial.

Because a required decision is needed and imminent, This Or That can still be very difficult for many reasons:

- Even with only two options, those that have difficulty making decisions may still struggle—two options may feel no different than five options.
- Getting to two "good" options could make the decision more difficult. This is the belief that all the "bad" options have been eliminated and the final two good options each make a compelling case.
- There could be a feeling that you let go of a good option that did not make the final two.
- Even at fifty-percent odds, deciding one way or the other, you may still not like your chances with the decision that you make.

None of these feelings or reactions are uncommon in the process of making decisions, so if you have experienced this, you are quite normal. The choices you must make should challenge you to think introspectively and to think about the impact of your selection. Getting down to two options is critical as the more that you must process in making the decision, the higher the potential risk of a poor outcome. Even the process itself could take too long. So:

This Or That is about simplifying your decision-making down to two options.

When a conflict occurs with decision-making, choices, or even prioritization, at times it can be traced back to the fact that there were too many options. When you can refine your options to two: This Or That, a few things can happen:

- You increase your odds of making the right choice or decision to at least fifty percent. Of course, fifty percent one way or the other. Think of holding a small ball in your hand. Then you ask someone to choose which hand is holding the ball. If you are an optimist, it is a fifty-percent possibility of being right, if you are a pessimist, a fifty-percent possibility of being wrong. No matter how much you agonize over which hand to choose, the odds are not going to change.

- You have likely narrowed a decision down to the two options that make the most sense... also increasing the odds that you will be satisfied with either one of your choices. By now, the "bad" options are gone, so you should feel good about whichever option you choose.

- You increase your chances of deciding faster with fewer things from which to choose. This should hold true in most cases. If it doesn't, then there are other things to consider that are slowing you down in your decision-making process.

Again, while getting your decision-making down to two options, This Or That is the goal, it doesn't always make the decision more straightforward; but it does at least increase your odds of a right decision. However, there is still an emotional or human element to consider.

One situation that I faced demonstrated the challenges that can complicate the decision, even when you have refined the process to two options.

I had a regional director approach me a few years ago about

how to handle a situation with a new store opening. This store was going to be a high-profile location with visibility to all the senior leaders who lived close to the store. Typically, the district manager would make this decision, but considering the importance of it, the regional director needed to be involved.

The decision that this leader was struggling with was about who to place in this store as the store manager when the new location opened.

The first order of business for me was to find out who the regional director was considering for store manager of this location. To my surprise, she had seven people that she was contemplating.

My recommendation to this leader was to identify criteria that would allow her to eliminate some of the choices available to her, which would eventually allow her to get down to two choices.

I walked her through a series of questions to gain a better understanding: we discussed what would be the anticipated volume of the store, the experience of the team that the store manager would be leading, the length of time each person being considered had been a store manager, if at all, and even how long each candidate had been with the company. As she answered each of those questions, the criteria began to separate the candidates, and she was able to get closer to the decision about who the final two candidates would be.

After those cursory questions, I went deeper:

Who would have the temperament for leading a new team? Who

would have the temperament for leading a store that was going to be scrutinized by corporate executives daily? What did she expect the customer base of the store to be like and who would be best skilled to serve them? Who would be willing to take the store and manage it for years and potentially forgo a promotion so that we had leadership stability in this critical store?

These questions changed the dynamic. It was no longer just about the functional aspect of managing the store. It was now about the emotional aspect of managing and leading.

At the beginning of the process, a case could be made for each of the possible selections, and many of them she was fond of. But by using both dimensions of criteria, it allowed the leader to eliminate candidates and arrive at a more balanced decision.

Also, going through this process provided specific data points to make conversations more productive with each candidate later as to why they were not selected.

While the process was difficult, the regional director was able to narrow the decision down to two choices. She felt great about the final two candidates. In fact, she felt equally great about both.

While there was plenty of criteria to separate these two choices for the store manager role from the other five candidates already eliminated, it still did not necessarily account for the human element.

There is another aspect of decision-making that process cannot solve, and that is intuition. Even when getting to a final pair of options to choose from, the tiebreaker may be good old-fashioned intuition, how you feel about your options given that all other criteria is considered equal.

In this specific case, intuition is what the regional director had to rely on as the tiebreaker for the final decision. The difference, however, is that she did not apply intuition when she had seven candidates to choose from. If so, she very well could have come to a different conclusion on who to select. In the end, though, a balance between emotion and analytics can help you get to the most completely-thought-out decision possible.

There's another example of a decision in which I was involved many years ago. I worked in an organization where we were deciding on where to host a leadership conference. We were determined to select a city that had a need where we could go in with a large group and make a difference in the community. We had four cities in the final conversation that all had an emotionally compelling story.

We agonized over it for weeks before making a decision. In reflection, part of the challenge for the team around the table is that we continued to look at data and all the pluses and minuses for four different cities. It was exhausting, and it felt difficult each time to contrast all of them—it was simply too many choices.

We discovered that we were treating the process as though all four cities had an equally compelling need. There is a theme here; we will discuss equal choices in a later chapter.

When we began to force ourselves to eliminate one of the four cities from consideration, we made some traction. The same occurred when we removed another one to get down to the final two cities.

Simply changing the way that we looked at the situation made a difference. Specifically, instead of focusing on which one of the four that we should choose, we concentrated on the one that we were least likely to select. We used quantitative data like the average income, population growth, and other socioeconomic factors to identify the city with the least amount of need. The process of elimination also worked for the next least likely city to select.

While deciding between the final two cities was not simple, we found that we exhausted less energy due to fewer choices, and we could think and process the decision with greater clarity.

You may be wondering why we didn't just start with the quantitative data. While we had the data available from the outset, we took the opposite approach from the example with the regional director selecting a store manager. We found ourselves appealing first to the emotional aspect of each of these cities that had needs for outside support. Because so much of this effort was about the community, how we would connect to each of them emotionally was high on the list of importance. When we could not seem to reach a decision based on emotion, the data helped us push through.

Making decisions using emotion is one of the most significant challenges that you can face. Emotions are, by definition, not rational, factual, or logical, therefore they can cause you to overlook key criteria and data that is available to you.

Again, the takeaway here is that making a balanced decision requires the data aspect and the emotional aspect.

The choices that you need to make in your personal life may be no easier — even small decisions.

I think back about every time we were trying to decide as a family where to eat dinner. As our children were growing up, we ate out far more often than the average family. You would think that over time, we would get better at our selection process, but we didn't. Having the philosophy of This Or That applied to the decision-making process at the time would have been helpful.

As I was usually the designated driver, the designated go-pick-it-up person, and of course, always the designated payer, I thought many times that this decision was going to be the death of me.

So how did we resolve this on most days? Painfully would be the correct answer. In reflection, we started from a universe of all restaurants. Of course, we would have been better served asking more qualifying questions to get ourselves to a manageable list of restaurants and then ultimately deciding on This Or That.

Far too many days, I ended up doing the dreaded "double-stop." You know, two people wanting one food choice and the other three wanting another. So, off I went making multiple stops when it was a carryout night. Even worse, if we were headed to a restaurant to eat, we would stop at one restaurant and pick up food to take with us to eat at the next restaurant. Anyone that is a parent of multiple small children knows about this experience.

Through using some straightforward filters, we could have dramatically reduced our number of choices each time. I am not sure that the process would have always narrowed us down to one restaurant that satisfied everyone, but at least a better process could have gotten us to two restaurants quicker.

Of course, I could have taken direction about This Or That from a former business colleague from my time working in the video industry, not only for my personal food dilemma, but also for broader business decision-making purposes.

Bob was a franchisee of Blockbuster Video. He also owned other businesses, specifically an advertising firm and a beauty business. Bob lived in the Midwest and managed all his businesses there.

It was a pivotal time in our business model at Blockbuster, and we were about to embark on game trading. As new game formats were emerging, a backload of game inventories accumulated in households. Many gamers no longer had use for the older formats. The ability to trade the game in for cash could benefit the customer and the business. To that end, I was told that I needed to visit Bob and get his opinion about the proposition, so I did. I got on a plane and went to see Bob in Kansas City.

As I was flying into town, the plane circled downtown Kansas City on the way to the airport. There I saw a building with a name on it that said "Bernstein." I thought that was a strange coincidence, as that was Bob's last name. As I got into the taxi to go meet Bob, it appeared that Bob's office was downtown as I could see the skyline coming into view bit by bit. As we got closer, it also became apparent that the multi-story building that I saw from the plane with the last name Bernstein on it was no coincidence—that was *his* building.

I first met with his son, Steve, then other key leaders and finally with Bob later in the day. It seemed somewhat like a gangster movie scene—someone taking me to meet the guy that would take me to the guy that would take me to the guy—minus the violence, of course.

I learned on that day that Bob was a pretty big deal. Bob showed me around his building—the floor that housed the video business, the level that housed the beauty business and the floor dedicated to his advertising firm. However, there were many other floors in the building that were overrun with, the only way that I can describe it is: pretty much one of everything in the world. Bob had collected so many things from his travels and businesses that he literally didn't know where to put it all—from baby grand pianos to well, everything else.

All that said, Bob's eclectic nature was not the most important thing that I learned on that trip.

Even with all the collections of stuff, Bob and his team were incredibly efficient in their business. I watched as they made calculated decisions in the moment about equipment, space, and planning for future growth. There were two in-the-moment decisions that happened while we were touring the building. I watched as there was a decision about ordering movies for the following week and about a pricing promotion in the beauty salons. With each situation, I found that there was early due diligence that the teams had been conditioned to utilize.

As Bob and his son, Steve, were showing me around, we were intercepted on our walk to make these two decisions. Bob and Steve were presented with a clear This Or That choice, and each was backed with facts and potential outcomes. It took longer for the scenario to be laid out than it did for Bob and Steve to make a decision. It was a credit to the level of efficiency and trust that they had built over time and a clear example of effective decision-making. Bob and his leaders only allowed themselves to be presented with This Or That decisions—time was too valuable for any more than that.

Oh, the other thing that I learned that day was about the advertising firm and its claim to fame. The advertising firm was Bob's pride and joy. His face beamed as he discussed the business.

Bob only had two clients in the beginning—they just happened to be the biggest burger chain in the world and the biggest overall retail business in the world- McDonald's and Wal-Mart, respectively.

As the McDonald's story goes, Bob was contacted by a regional ad manager for the golden arches company. Bernstein, whose advertising firm handled McDonald's restaurants in the Midwest and Southwest, had already been working on a kid's meal.

Bob said: "I came up with the Happy Meal in 1975, as I watched my son, Steve, at the breakfast table reading his cereal box. He did it every morning. We could make a box for McDonald's that holds a meal and gives kids things to do."

At a meeting with franchise owners, Bernstein heard that moms needed something simple to handle, and restaurant owners wanted to streamline the ordering of kids' food. So, Bob began trademarking cups, plates, and lids as "Happy Cups," "Happy Plates," etc. He made a deal with Keebler for cookies; he hired children's book illustrators and graphic designers to work on a box.

There has been a debate as others have laid claim to creating the Happy Meal. There could be some truth to other claims, but no matter, Bernstein perfected the idea.

Before McDonald's agreed to make the Happy Meal a national product, Bernstein's Happy Meals were being tested and advertised for a couple of years in Kansas City, Phoenix, and Denver. Bob and his firm even trademarked the Happy Meal name.

During the summer of 1979, McDonald's premiered the Happy Meal nationally. The first boxes were circus wagons. The first toys were tops, stencils, wallets, puzzles, and erasers. And initially, meals included a hamburger or cheeseburger, fries, a soft drink, and cookies.

So, there you go –Bob Bernstein of Kansas City, created the Happy Meal.

Oh, his firm also coined the term "Make It A Blockbuster Night" for Blockbuster in the early '90s. Pretty cool—efficient decision-maker and innovator too.

My digression to discuss the Happy Meal is not random. It brings us to another essential point about This Or That and intuition.

As it relates to the Happy Meal, Bob worked on a straightforward principle. "Your five-year-old child decides where you are going to eat." I am confident that if I said this in a room full of parents, I would get lots of heads nodding and I am certain that if I understood and embraced this as my children were growing up, perhaps I would have had fewer "double-stops."

As it relates to This Or That decision-making, intuition plays a pivotal role, particularly as you get to two tough options that appear to be equal in value. I saw Bob use intuition as we walked the halls of his building making decisions, and as he described watching his son, Steve, eat cereal and read the box. Bob appealed to the connection and the emotion of his son with the box—that was intuition not only as a leader, but also as a father.

Many leaders are paralyzed when it comes to making decisions. There will be times when your choices appear to be equal and intuition will save the day.

I will say this—if you are having difficulty making decisions in your personal life, especially small decisions, you will have challenges making decisions in a leadership role inside of an organization.

It is admirable to believe that you can show up at work, put on a cape, and be someone else. It is not likely to happen, at least not consistently over time.

So, back to This Or That. You do need to reach a point of comfort in the decision-making process that allows you to limit yourself to two options, and confidently make a decision. A couple of additional things to consider:

- Limit yourself to the two options that you have in front of you. If you find yourself wanting to consider an additional alternative not available, then you have not accepted the two choices that are in front of you, or it could also be that your process of getting to the final two options is flawed.
- When you cannot reduce your number of choices down to two, focus on eliminating one at a time and reasoning why you wouldn't choose that option. Follow that process until you get to two choices.
- Once you get to two choices, a decision still must be made, but you have gotten as close as you can get without making the final decision.

Once you begin to feel confident that you have reduced your choices down to the final two and your decision-making is becoming more refined, it is then time to apply it to an important decision in your organization or even to an important personal decision that perhaps you have been putting off.

In conjunction with demonstrating self-discipline and using Or instead of And, This Or That should prepare you to simplify your environment.

CHAPTER 9:

The Road To Simplification

Complexity. Whenever this word is used to describe a process, design, or business strategy, you may feel like everything around you is chaotic and out of control. Indeed, by definition, complexity can cause conflict and abnormal mental behavior.

In our current world with increasingly global operations, diverse workforces, shorter product cycles, omnichannel expansion, and empowered customers, complexity seems to be unavoidable.

Of course, it can be avoided. This chapter is placed ahead of the chapter on prioritization because I believe that:

Before you can get to effective prioritization, you must get to effective simplification.

For the sake of this conversation, think of simplification as the process of removing the things that are not real priorities. Therefore, simplification needs to happen before prioritization.

Additionally, think of simplification as unbundling the complexities that prevent you and your people from getting maximum productivity and results. Indeed, that can be applied to your personal life as well.

Let me say more about complexity. Complexity is often self-inflicted. Take our current-day situation of information flow. The negative impact that information flow has on today's business and productivity should not be underestimated. The amount of information that leaders must react to, whether it requires action or not, has reached a tipping point.

Tipping point? I know, that sounds like a strong word choice... that is because it is... intentionally. There are no longer any boundaries for communication, information requests or information sharing. As more information has been shared and become more accessible, so has the expectation of a response... a quick response. Complexity has created undue, unnecessary and unregulated stress.

Let's face it, any part of our personal life without boundaries comes with risks, so any aspect of business without boundaries is subject to the same type of risks.

The overwhelming amount of information that we process is causing complexity and confusion and leaving many of us believing that we have no other choice but to accept the Power Of And.

The first step is to acknowledge and truly believe that complexity is self-inflicted. If something is self-inflicted, that means that you have control over it and the likelihood of being able to undo the complexity is greater. This will get you on your way to simplification, but there is more to consider.

Too often in business, every priority is justified as being important, and you can never quite get to what is *most* important. This is where simplification becomes critical.

However, simplification sometimes gets a bad rap. Simplification does not mean easy, and it does not mean doing the least amount possible.

To be effective, we must fully understand simplification and even oversimplification—too little of the former and too much of the latter and optimal success may not be achieved.

I have seen many examples in organizations of over-engineering for success. Planning is a vital part of success, but if you spend more time planning than taking action, you are likely cutting into your probability of success, for no other reason than the lack of time spent toward delivering on the plan itself to drive success.

Simplification is not terribly difficult, but it can be overlooked as a key to success because, frankly, it is not complicated.

Many of us are taught from an early age statements like: most things in life are not free and most things that we want we must work hard to get. Also, let me throw in, if it looks too good to be true, then it probably is.

I suppose skepticism is a prerequisite to becoming an adult. Perhaps, we work harder than we need to at times as a result of beliefs like these that are instilled in us, usually with good intentions by our parents.

Our conditioning at times has been such that we don't believe a simple solution when we see it. We begin looking for more-the trick, the "catch," what is "behind the curtain." Perhaps, that type of thinking is needed at times; I'm not sure that using a skeptical filter and expecting complexity is a strong default position. It feels a bit exhausting as well.

I have worked for organizations in large-scale operations with hundreds, even thousands of stores in my scope. In support of those stores, I have watched senior leaders work very hard to solve problems at store level by creating processes and programs that were complex, expensive, and time-consuming to deploy.

In almost every example where these large-scale programs were created and deployed, there was a simple solution that was never addressed. Again, simplification doesn't mean easy, but simplification should mean identifying the straightest and most impactful path to success.

I worked for a company for years that created program after program from the headquarters designed to improve the life of the store managers and the experience of the customers. Of course, all were constructed with good intentions.

Often, we did not get traction with new programs, particularly those that involved a behavior change in the store. It was challenging to determine what the common denominators were when things did not work out. What I eventually learned over the years is that the common denominators had nothing to do with processes, tools, the time of the year, or conflicts with other priorities.

It was about the hostility of change management and it was about the competence of the leader, the store manager.

It was not surprising to me to see many of these programs never work due to a hostile response to change management, sometimes overt and sometimes passive aggressive. That is a topic for another book simply because change management is an expansive subject that needs its own book.

To that end, the key to implementing real, sustainable change is that the leader must buy into it. When the store manager did not believe in the change, it didn't matter what we did from the headquarters- change didn't happen.

In other situations, the store manager was simply not capable of executing the plan. When there were turnover issues in the store, you could trace them back to the leader—poor scheduling, posting schedules late, not scheduling to employees' availability, manager not working their hours and the team feeling like they were working harder than their leader. The list goes on and on, but all related to the environment that the store manager was creating.

Of course, when results were not achieved in a store, that

was an even more tangible way to trace the gap back to the manager's lack of leadership.

I believe that leadership teams may find it counterintuitive to look at easy solutions only due to the belief that problems are complex to solve.

So often, you hear people say that if it were that easy, everyone would be doing it. Perhaps, the people doing it realized that there was a simple way while the rest of us were making it complicated.

There are plenty of examples of how the world around us has become more complex. What you must consider in your personal life and as a leader is how much of that complexity is self-inflicted.

I certainly do not profess that simplification is easy. As evidence, the lack of simplification exists in all parts of our lives. I am a sports fan and, even in that space, I have found an absence of simplification.

For example, I have always found it fascinating to watch (NFL) National Football League coaches (pick almost any of them), standing on the sideline with a huge laminated card in their hand that holds around 200 plays. These cards are usually held in front of the coach's face as they call the play as though they would be divulging the secrets of the universe if someone could read their lips. Even more concerning is that most NFL teams have somewhere in the range of 400-500 total plays and by a process, reduce the number to around 200 plays for game day.

In the end, the average team may only run about eighty plays during a game, and some plays are run more than once, so possibly only fifty unique plays run for the entire game. So, depending on the play usage, a team may not use all their plays well into the season!

To take it a step further, some NFL coaches have added another layer of complexity by scripting out their first fifteen to twenty plays of the game, without regard for what the game situation may dictate.

In this situation, an effective coach may be better served to run the first seven to eight scripted plays and make adjustments if they are not seeing success, rather than stay with the pre-determined scripted plays. Okay, now I'm playing arm-chair quarterback.

The play development and play scripting is just a microcosm of the more significant issue that I see in football, and that is the self-inflicted complexity.

Every year, the NFL holds its draft for teams to select players from college and about that time, there are multiple talking heads on each network saying the same things over and over: the NFL game is much faster than the college game, the playbooks are much more complex, the defensive schemes are much more intricate, blah, blah, blah.

I do not question whether that is true or not. What I wonder is whether there is ownership by coaches, general managers, and owners that they have done this to themselves. When I grew up playing football, we only had about ten plays, and we all knew them well after the first week of practice. I realize with this statement I sound like my father. The fact is, the game of football worked well when it was simple, and it also works well now with more complexity. So, with all things being equal, it would seem logical to choose simple.

So, what is the point in all of this?

Well, two things.

We often choose complexity; it doesn't choose us.

Also, we don't always think about the benefits of simplification or, said differently; we do not always think about the downside of complexity.

In the example of having 400-500 plays, consider the amount of time that players must sit in a film room and with their playbook day and night learning plays that they may never run. This should make coaches pause and question how much more productive their players could be by spending their time doing something more important.

A third point to take away from this, not specific to sports, is that we often find comfort in mass.

The more we have of something or the more choices, can make us feel more comfortable about having an option to fit every outcome.

This may make you feel better about the decisions that you are making, but it will not help you with simplification.

My apologies to the readers who do not follow sports, but I am going to stick with sports on another example as well that ties into the conversation about simplification.

I recently attended a Houston Astros baseball game. I was watching the players getting ready for the game, and the batting coach was hitting baseballs to players standing in the outfield. The players caught every single one of the balls. In fact, a major league outfielder will likely catch 99 or 100 out of 100 baseballs hit to them. Ninety-nine percent is very realistic and expected at that level.

However, if you start hitting two balls simultaneously to a major league outfielder, the catch percentage will drop dramatically. The outfielder must choose instantaneously which one to catch, and the laser focus on one baseball has been broken.

Even the most talented outfielder might only catch both balls half of the time, depending on how close the balls are hit to each other.

Perhaps this example is more exaggerated than what happens in a business setting when a new priority is added to the mix, but it depends on how significant the priority is that is being added and the priorities that you are already working on. I will describe it this way. In a business setting, it does not involve the same physical demand as in the example of the baseball outfielder, but it certainly can be an equivalent mental demand. Again, complexity creates abnormal psychological behavior.

In the baseball example, the player and his ability have not changed at all, but the environment around him has... dramatically.

This takes us to my position on *ability versus capability*. I believe that:

Ability is 'can you do it?' Capability is 'can you do it... under the circumstances?'

This is a critical principle as it relates to simplification.

Examining this a bit further, the definition of capability has the word ability in it. Now that seems confusing. However, the definition of ability is related to the word capability. Perhaps I am reading too much into this. However, both words have 'capacity' as a synonym—another word overused in the corporate world.

I acknowledge that right now, I am arguing against my own point and proving that the words are more similar than dissimilar in definition.

Ability and capability are, in fact, similar, until you get to a leadership application of each of them.

From a talent perspective, ability is often misdiagnosed in organizations.

On many occasions, just because a person is not considered successful in a role, the tendency is to believe that the person is not able to do the job. It may be that, given the situation, with the circumstances that have been created, nobody could do the job.

Capability allows for a very loose, maybe better described

as a lazy approach, to talent planning. Describing one's top organizational talent as not having the capability to do the job can be a way to avoid the responsibility of identifying specific competency deficiencies—like time management, planning and organizing, communication, etc. It can also be a way to avoid the responsibility of setting the person up for success. Using the capability umbrella is basically a way out for those who are leading the talent planning process.

I submit that capability is not a competency.

If you apply the capability definition to the baseball outfielder example, he would likely be assessed as no longer able to play at the professional level and be sent down to the minor leagues to improve. The reality is that his skill was still top-level, but the environment or circumstances around him had changed so dramatically that he could no longer perform at an acceptable level.

Therefore, simplification is significant. When complexity is added to any situation, it can cause a misdiagnosis and especially as it relates to talent. It is easy to miss the complexity component and focus elsewhere to solve the problem.

When you apply this to organizational priorities, it can have an impact financially. This can also lead to the changing of executive leaders by the board or other oversight structure, only to find that the next executive leaders are beset with the same challenges. A vicious cycle begins because the assessment is focused on capability instead of ability.

So, what to do with this?

You can start by getting rid of unnecessary rules, low-value activities, and timewasters that exist in abundance in your organization or in your personal life.

Let me start on the personal side. Lack of organization in your personal life will no doubt creep into your professional life and impact your ability to be successful on the job.

If you feel like you have too much to do in your personal life, it indeed could be a capability discussion that you need to have with yourself. Perhaps no one can do what it is that you are attempting to do.

I think it's particularly important to assess those things in your personal life that you believe you were once good at doing and no longer feel adequately able to do. There is a high probability that you still can do those things, but something in your environment has changed that is preventing you from being able to feel successful. That something could be more obvious like a significant life change—marriage, divorce, having children. On the contrary, it could be something simple, straightforward, and yet not as easily detectable.

For example, let's consider cleaning your house. What used to take you an hour to complete is now a two-hour project. You may be moving as quickly as you did years ago, but during that time you moved from living in an apartment to living in a house twice the size. You may not have bought any additional clothing that requires washing or purchased any extra furniture or tables that need to be cleaned. You may have even gained some efficiencies with new cleaners and equipment that is available now and yet you feel less productive than before.

Of course, you may find that you're taking more time to do things like checking your phone throughout the process of cleaning and that alone could be extending your cleaning by an additional twenty minutes. Your phone can be an incredible productivity tool, but your phone can also be the ultimate timewaster.

Again, your ability may not have changed at all, but your capability could be very different --the circumstances have shifted enough to have an impact on your overall productivity.

I am purposely selecting a task as mundane as cleaning your house because these are things that we take for granted as we go through our daily and weekly routines. So much so, that it may be the last place that we look to assess our ability versus environmental changes affecting our capability. There are many other low-value activities and unnecessary rules that we impose on ourselves in our personal lives... even though we are ultimately our own boss.

On the business side of getting rid of low-value activities, assess processes, like something as simple as expense reports. Look at how many people need to review and sign off on expense reports or small purchases. I worked in an organization in which the president demanded that he had to sign off on travel for regional directors... four levels below him.

I often say that in business, not every idea is a good idea. This is one of those. Not only did this process speak to adding complexity and slowing down processes, but it also created an undercurrent of distrust in decision-making. The intention was pure—it was to deter travel and influence leaders, up to four levels below, to only spend on business-critical activities, submit fewer expense reports, and ultimately reduce the number of expenses incurred by the organization.

There are layers of issues to examine when unnecessary rules are put in place that directly undercut simplification: three of them are communication, process, and outcomes.

From a communication perspective, this expense report policy was implemented without any purview by other leaders. So, not only was it a surprise to the regional director level, but it was also a surprise to their leaders, who frankly could not adequately explain or defend the new policy.

From a process perspective, this was a significant change and not a welcome change for trust reasons already mentioned. It also meant precious time leaders could spend leading was being diverted to administrative work. While it might have been only an additional fifteen to twenty minutes per week, that time begins to be substantive as it aggregates over weeks and months and among so many leaders.

Lastly, from an outcome perspective, we did reduce our expense run rate by seven percent over the next six months. However, we found that we may have sacrificed some tradeoffs in the process. Due to a reduction in travel, we had lost some of our connection to the field, and due to a reduction in meetings, particularly related to the limited travel, we saw a decrease in execution.

To be balanced in this conversation, the process of an additional approval of expense reports is not particularly complicated; however, simplification is a matter of perspective.

Doing something more, anything more than what you were required to do before can give the feeling of moving from simple to complex.

Conversely, if you can identify processes that can be improved by eliminating unnecessary rules, ones that today seem complicated in your organization, you can realize the benefit of your teams feeling like something complicated or complex has been removed. This can boost morale and productivity.

In another situation, I worked in an organization that was having issues with supply costs. To address the problem, the organization required all orders of supplies to be called in for approval to the regional director for the next quarter with the intent to reduce supply costs by five percent. This process took the responsibility completely from the store manager, skipped over the district manager, and slowed down the process. In the end, the good news is that the five percent savings was achieved as planned.

However, two things happened. The quarter following the savings, the supply costs jumped back up—yes, you guessed it—by five percent. Also, the trust of the store managers had been broken as they no longer felt empowered to manage their store since they could not even order toilet paper without approval—a true story and true sentiments.

So, policies that add complexity and bureaucracy need to go. Good intentions are not good enough to deliver good business. You need fundamentally sound decision-making, and that also means, at times, just keeping it simple or making it simple.

And oh, one more thing, stop being so nice.

This applies to any level of leadership within an organization.

One of the patterns that causes or exacerbates complexity inside of organizations is the tendency for people to not speak up about poor practices. This is especially true when people hesitate to challenge more senior leaders who may unintentionally create complexity through poor meeting management, unclear assignments, unnecessary emails, or other poor managerial habits.

I fundamentally believe that most people want to be told the truth. Yes, I know very well the line uttered by Jack Nicholson's character from the movie, A Few Good Men, "You can't handle the truth!"

Here is what I will say about that—I believe that we suppress more than we should. I think that there are times when we believe we have spoken up only to find that we have just said it over and over so many times in our head that it gave us the illusion that we had said it out loud.

I'm not sure if most of us can handle the truth because I am not sure that we hear the truth often enough to recognize it and productively respond to it. However, learning the truth can unlock problems and make real, sustainable change happen.

This is important context for this discussion because leaders that ascend to the top of organizations hear less "truth" the higher they go. They are often placated by people around them, we call them "yes" people, and the leader can develop a false sense of how things are going in their organization.

Whether you are a leader in a large, mid-size, or small organization, it is all relative. Most structures and spans of control are similar enough that, no matter the size of the company, you have a similar amount of direct reports and people above and below you to whom you must report. So, there is always a mechanism in which you can call out unnecessary complexity. Simplification can be executed in organizations of any size.

Stepping away from the corporate world, I have had the advantage of replaying conversations that I've heard or participated in, and I have gained new context from them.

For example, I heard one executive describing why it was hard for their organization to make a change. He used the analogy that a small company is like a sailboat, very agile. At a moment's notice, the captain can pivot and change directions rather quickly. However, he referred to a larger organization as an ocean liner—much more weight causing it to take much more time to change course.

In the larger organization example, when a leader wants to make a change, it is a much slower and methodical process to slow the ocean liner down, to make the hook around and change directions. His point more directly is change cannot happen as quickly in a larger organization. At that time, it made a lot of sense and I bought into it. But as I reflect on it now, that's all bullshit.

There is another step in the simplification journey, and this is an important one—you must ask the question:

"What should we stop doing?"

It seems like a simple enough question, and yet it is one that often stops teams in their tracks. This question can shut down an organization. Okay, perhaps that is a bit exaggerated, but this point cannot be given too much emphasis. Most organizations don't know where to begin in terms of answering the question of what they should stop doing. So, they don't.

I worked with a senior leader years ago who said something that has always stuck with me. She said, "We don't ever kill anything, we just stun it." Her reference, of course, was about projects and initiatives that came up to which we could never say no. Consequently, the marketing, operations, and IT activity calendars would be overloaded; and when we were pushed in a corner to eliminate something, we would move it to the next quarter or the next fiscal year. Guess what was waiting there? More work that we had already pushed to the next quarter or the next fiscal year.

The first time that she shared her one-liner, and every time after that, she always got a laugh from the room. You know what is said about comedy though—there is some level of truth in every joke. So, to this point, we all often laughed at the statement, but we also knew it was true. The fact that there was truth to it was an indictment of us as an organization.

But wait, it may not be a simple question. It can be complicated, based on:

- the needs of the business
- where the business is in its lifecycle
- the tenure of the team working together
- whether the company is public or private
- the financial situation of the company
- the priorities that have capital already allocated

Any of this sound familiar? Good...

...now forget about all of them. Every one of these challenges that I just presented are nothing but excuses.

The point of this is that almost everything that we do can be justified, reasonably justified, or not. In business, getting the work done is what you are ultimately judged by and creating more work than you can complete can create so many different and new problems—headaches such as reverting to multitasking, lack of focus, low employee morale and potentially completing work that was not the most important work to complete.

I applaud leadership teams that dare to ask the question of what they should stop doing.

Unfortunately, most organizations don't make it to the finish line of clearly identifying those things to stop doing and then actually follow through on it. To do it takes courage. Perhaps more than what is needed in any other part of your business.

Back to the point earlier in this chapter:

Before you can get to effective prioritization, you must get to effective simplification.

Clearing the decks, so to speak, with simplification will help you in your personal life and you may earn more credibility with your team in your leadership role. You are now ready to prioritize.

CHAPTER 10:

The Road To Prioritization

Prioritization- perhaps the only word in business more complicated than the word complexity discussed in the previous chapter. Everyone wants to know what the priorities are. How many, in what order, and when they need to be delivered. If it were that simple, there would not be a need for this chapter. However, there is a need for this chapter.

Again, simplification must occur before you can get to prioritization. If you are attempting to prioritize thirty-seven initiatives, to that I say, good luck. There is a belief in some leadership teams that they can rank all their priorities and then attempt to get them all done, no matter the obstacles.

The title of this book is The Power Of Or, so you already know how I feel about that belief.

One of the most significant gaps related to priorities is remembering that there is work that needs to be done behind each of them. The activities, or "click-downs" (note corporate buzzword) associated with completing one priority can be taxing on an organization and its people. These activities must be carried out by real people with varying degrees of abilities.

Let's start from the beginning. The word priority did not always mean what it does today. The word priority entered the English language around the 1400s, and, at the time, it was singular. It meant the very first or prior thing. The word priority remained singular for the next five hundred years.

In the 1900s, leaders decided to pluralize the term, and we started talking about priorities. We believed that by changing the word, we could somehow change reality and ultimately change capacity. We would now be able to create an environment where multiple things were all first or the priority.

While this gave the impression of many things being the priority, it meant that nothing was, according to the spirit of the definition of priority.

Perhaps this is not as drastic as the ideas of creating an alternate universe; but in a business context, it is almost the equivalent.

Even in the present day, the definition of priority still identifies it as a thing that is regarded as more important than another.

Now, in the twenty-first century, we believe that we have reached a new level of sophistication that allows us to do more and have more priorities than ever before. We have become skilled at the strategic plan, the annual operating plan, the multi-year strategy, the transformational agenda, the global agenda and so many other monikers used to describe a ridiculous amount of work that is planned which cannot possibly be executed in a reasonable timeframe and by mere human beings.

Prioritization is not simple. Organizations spend significant amounts of money and human capital to defend, I mean define their priorities (Freudian slip) —offsite retreats with executive coaches, strategy specialists brought in to create activities geared toward pointing everyone in the same direction and enough tools and processes designed to make your head spin.

Prioritization doesn't have to be that scientific. Prioritization cannot be that scientific. It must be practical and realistic—that is if you expect it to be bought into and executed by the people working in your organization.

Let's start with this. There are many maxims related to prioritization. Here are a few:

- Everything cannot be as important as everything else. If that is your situation, those are not priorities. That is called a checklist.
- Your environment may change often, and there must be a declaration that something has moved up or down on the priority list. If you don't check and adjust, you may be expending a lot of energy and getting nothing done in return.
- Because something was once deemed a priority, doesn't make it a priority forever.
- The impact or value of doing each thing on your priority

list is different. This should help you determine the order of work.

Just applying these fundamental maxims may help you avoid some very basic pitfalls of prioritization.

I will share one of the pitfalls that I experienced many years ago, only weeks after we had built our strategic plan for the upcoming fiscal year. It was a clear indication that we were *not* on the right path to real prioritization. I only need to say this:

1A, 1B, 1C.

If you have gone through any level of a priority planning process, you get this.

Many years ago, I worked with a director named Rachel who believed that she could manipulate the priorities. Rachel would take the priorities from the executive team and put her twist on them. 'Twist' meaning that she would tuck in a priority of her own and call it 1A, or 1B or 1C as a way of keeping the same number of priorities while adding additional areas of focus. When this happened, I saw most people around the table laugh about it. It was clever. It was witty, but it was not funny.

That approach has been the running joke in many organizations, but in the end, it is not very funny if it causes you to lose sales and profits due to lack of discipline and prioritization as well as the frustration that it can cause among your teams.

There must be prioritization at the highest level—priorities that everyone supports. When that is not defined and honored, the likelihood of clear focus and execution is diminished. Also, the whispers begin among your teams and, in the end, you lose credibility as a leader or leadership team.

From the agreed-upon key priorities, of course, there could be critical assignments that fall within the scope of a department, perhaps what Rachel was attempting to define. However, if that work does not link to the overall priorities, and if it puts the agreed-upon priorities at risk of failure, then there needs to be a process which calls that out.

I will share that, in my experience, it is also essential to identify the next level of activities to support those key strategic priorities.

This may sound counterintuitive and even contradictory to what I discussed in the previous chapter about simplification. I agree, but the difference is that we are now talking about only the priorities that matter, so it is not only okay to go more in-depth defining the work to support those priorities, it is vital to do so for the sake of your teams.

Why? In my experience, I have seen too many examples of the strategic priorities being so strategic that, without identifying the next level of activities to support them, any work that is done in the organization can be justifiably tucked under one of those strategic priorities. So, leaving the strategic priorities entirely open for interpretation can create just as many problems as having too many priorities. 1A, 1B, 1C is not always an intentional act. Nonetheless, you end up in the same place as the example with Rachel.

Prioritization can be tricky-tricky because the understanding of the organization's ability to execute can and usually does look different from the top of the organization versus the front line of the organization.

Many times, the executive leader or executive team will find nuanced ways to tuck in more work than the frontline teams believe is possible to deliver. This is sometimes necessary, but the line is very fine, and it is the responsibility of the organizational leadership to know where that line exists.

I worked with a leader many years ago whom I will call Jeff. He became frustrated with his leadership team because of their frustration that the organization had too many priorities. Not only was the feedback coming from Jeff's leadership team, but it was also coming from the field organization. However, this leader had isolated himself in such a way that there was no voice in his ear inside of the organization—no one that had the ability to give him the ground truth about what was happening. It is a potentially dangerous place for any leader or organization to be in.

Whether there was real merit to the concerns that were raised by his team is hard to say or to prove, but the fact that it was such a universal dissent seemed to validate that the team's basis of concern was real. At the very least, the concerns deserved to be heard.

Instead of exploring the concerns that were raised, Jeff got all his leaders together and their direct reports and proclaimed that they did not have too many priorities. Jeff did not listen to his leadership team or the feedback from the field. Instead, in that meeting, he doubled down on his position by challenging the team to call out specific items that they considered a low priority and therefore, should be eliminated.

In that moment and in that environment, regardless of title, tenure or leadership courage, you are not likely going to get anyone to step forward... and it did not happen on that day. If for no other reason than out of respect for the work done across other departments as represented in the room, no one wanted to call anyone else or their work out as being less important. I am sure each person had their reason for not speaking up that day, not the least of which was job security.

Unfortunately, the lack of anyone willing to voice their concerns at that moment only reinforced Jeff's position. He continued to push forward, and, to his credit, perhaps more work was completed in the organization than would have been without his pressured leadership approach.

Though the quality of the work was less of a concern to me, in retrospect, I don't believe the quality of the work was as good as it could have been. The real issue was employee morale. It was eroded on that day, and it took months, if not years, to restore confidence with many of the leaders in that room.

Being a part of the meeting that day, I wanted to shout out something, just one word—the word discipline. That's all that came to my mind as I listened to what turned into a lecture by this leader. If discipline were in place in that organization at the time and self-discipline was in place with Jeff, the morale of the teams and the productivity would have been different, and there would not have been a need for the meeting at all.

It was an important lesson for me and one that I have been reminded of with each step in my leadership journey as I have taken on more responsibility in my career.

I am going to share this one more time.

Discipline is essential. The higher you move up in an organization, the fewer the people to exact discipline on you as a leader. It then becomes an issue of self-discipline—you as a leader making tough decisions and tradeoffs with minimal prompting or guidance.

You can see how this point of prioritization now ties back to the self-discipline discussed earlier in the book.

When teams begin to believe that their leaders don't "get it," it can begin a snowball effect of dissent. There is a distinction here in this example: not knowing, not acknowledging, and not taking action are all separate issues that can influence the morale of teams.

Teams can and will give their leaders a break when they believe that the leader does not know of the challenges with which they are faced. It could be that there are no mechanisms in place for leaders to get that feedback, like engagement surveys and open forums. Teams may, however, find other ways to voice their concerns.

Not acknowledging concerns, as in the case with Jeff, is very dangerous. Minimalizing concerns or disputing them can create a significant disconnect.

Not taking action can also create problems; however, it is not always a negative thing. For example, a group of employees may be calling for a change in the bonus plan. The response may be a definite no and here is why it is not changing. While the group may be unhappy with the answer, they can at least acknowledge that the leaders were informed of the issue and addressed the issue.

Unfortunately, this one leader is not unique. I have worked with many other leaders who refused to prioritize; instead, they've said that everything is a priority, and it can all be done. Well, there are a whole host of issues inherent with that statement.

For starters, you must assess what you will have to give up for all this to happen. There is always something, and the best leaders will identify what that 'give-up' is and address it as they assess and assign their priorities. More than likely, when you overburden the organization, the 'give-up' has to do with your people.

If you believe in Theory Y, developed by Douglas McGregor at MIT in the 1960s, you could be putting the morale of your people at stake. Theory Y assumes that employees are ambitious, self-motivated, and anxious to accept greater responsibility and exercise self-control, self-direction, autonomy, and empowerment.

If you are experiencing negative morale in your organization, there are likely internal environmental factors that have caused it to occur as most employees begin their employment with you as Theory Y.

Second, you must think about how well you want all this work to be done—the quantity-versus-quality debate. Checking the box on multiple priorities related to important strategic work might satisfy a board or some other entity related to the organization, but it may have a negative effect on those that are inside of the organization.

Lastly, statements like "do-it-all" can make the leader appear out of touch with the teams that they are leading... especially when the team knows that the leader will likely not be doing most of the work. Such demonstrative statements can also close the door on employees, greatly reducing the possibility of employees giving you feedback or contrary evidence to consider.

If credibility matters to you as a leader, these are checkpoints that you should consider as part of your prioritization process.

So, what does real prioritization look like? It depends on the mission of the organization. You must understand what you are trying to accomplish and deliver to your constituents—employees, customers, shareholders, board members, etc. Much of it may depend on the structure of the organization. Whatever the structure, when setting priorities, it is essential to consider all who have a stake in the business.

This may sound like a non-answer, and that is because it is. Going into a strategic priority planning session with an outcome already in mind can be very dangerous. If the process is truly about the long-term success of the organization and its people, you owe it to yourself to be completely open about the expected outcomes.

One other point about priorities—they should be measurable. If you don't make your priorities measurable, the result will likely be the equivalent of my experience as a parent when my son came home from school at report card time. I can recall his response when I asked to see his report card. He said that the report cards were not ready, that there was a glitch in the system.

Of course, these "glitches" often happened, usually every six weeks. I proceeded to ask my son how he did on his report card. His response was "good." I could not do much with that response. Did that mean better than last time? Better than what he expected? Better than what I expected? Passing grades?

So yes, measurement is essential. Even if it is not important to you, it is likely vital to those around you, especially if you are a leader of people. Measurement can be a factor to help you slim your list of priorities. This applies whether it is a numerical measurement or a matrix approach, measuring things like high and low impact crossing with complexity or level of ease of implementation, etc.

Regardless of your choice of measurement, the number of priorities admitted to by an organization is revealing. As you evaluate your organization, you must ensure that there are no 1A, 1B, 1C priorities. It may be funny to discuss, but incredibly challenging to execute. Remember, everyone has the responsibility to call this out and ensure that the organization sticks to its priorities.

In my experience, the most successful executives tend to have a laser-like focus on a small number of priorities. These executives know what matters today and tomorrow: the more focus, the better.

At best, prioritizing enhances the strategic dialogue and the alignment at the top of the organization, from where it is cascaded to the rest of the organization. Once the executive team is aligned on this, priorities become a part of the organization and its corporate culture.

It also means that as a result of making these priorities clear, you are delivering a message that other things are not as important and, therefore, are not priorities.

If you are so inclined to rank your priorities, a couple of things should happen. First, you must ensure that you have the right criteria for your organization to rank them. Using incorrect criteria can lead to you to identifying activities as priorities that will not return the best value. Second, you need to decide on how many priorities you will have... and stick with it.

Strategic planning does not have to be boring, and it does not have to be complicated. In fact, it should not be complicated, and it is okay if it's boring.

Just remember, before you can get to effective prioritization, you must get to effective simplification.

CHAPTER 11:

The Scenario

I went through my own real-life exercise around simplification and prioritization.

Jamba Juice, one of the most recent organizations that I worked for, was going through a massive turnaround when I arrived in early 2017. I assure you, though, nothing about this situation would be simple.

It was an organization with a new leadership team. Jamba Juice was also in the process of relocating the headquarters and hiring all new talent because most people working in key positions would not relocate from San Francisco to Frisco, Texas—similar name, very different lifestyle to consider for many of them.

We were also moving to an asset-light model-selling company store markets to franchisees—and doing all this while being a public company. Oh, and we were mired in an audit that lasted more than a year. Other than all that, it was easy.

With this backdrop, the opportunity was compelling when the recruiter called. He did mention that it was a turnaround situation a few times during our conversation. I heard him, but I am not quite sure that I understood him. It would be unlike any other situation from my previous business experience.

I left Starbucks and came in as the chief operating officer with an expectation of focusing on operations, operations support, and training. I found myself doing much more work than that—some imposed and some self-inflicted.

About eight weeks into the role, my frustration level was already being tested. Mostly because the business model changes were complicated by our inability to focus on a few priorities and do them well, which was being driven by our complicated business model changes. You can begin to understand the vortex that we were in.

We did have five overarching strategic priorities that I believed were well-scripted and well-defined. However, a key learning point that I mentioned earlier through prior strategic planning sessions was: if you do not prescribe the first level of activities or tactics to support those overarching strategic priorities, you may find people in your organization justifying any work to fit under these pillars.

So, I went to the CEO and recommended that we have an offsite meeting for the leadership team, and I explained the reason why I felt it necessary. I wanted the executive team to get granular about our strategic priorities and discuss what is getting in our way. The CEO agreed, and we scheduled the offsite session for five weeks out.

When the time came, the seven of us on the executive team went offsite from the headquarters for two full days: our chief executive officer, our chief finance officer, chief marketing officer, chief systems officer, vice president of finance, general counsel, and me.

For my part, and since it was my insistence that the offsite meeting occur, I came prepared with scripted flipcharts that would help the process along. I must admit, I was very excited and optimistic—so much so, that I arrived early to prepare the room.

I posted flipcharts around the room with the following headers:

> What Does Success Look Like?
>
> Our Strategic Priorities
>
> How Do We Advance Our Strategy?
>
> Sacred Cows
>
> Red Herrings
>
> SWOT Analysis
>
> Roadblocks
>
> Are We Talking To Ourselves?
>
> What Will We Say No To?
>
> Priority Matrix (Stop/Start/Continue)

A lot to get to in two days for sure, but a fair representation of how many things needed clarification.

I realized that a layer of complexity added to this process upon which we were about to embark was that we hardly knew each other. The most tenured person on the executive team had been with the organization for four years. No one else around the table had been with the company beyond one year. That said, I do not believe that there was any distrust around the table, merely a lack of knowledge of each other.

To our credit, though, we had very committed professionals. While we came from other industries, we all understood the magnitude of what we were attempting to accomplish.

That said, the process began. We did an icebreaker that focused on learning about each other's leadership styles. We used one of the more familiar models, answered the questions, scored it, and discussed our different leadership styles. Frankly, not a lot of surprises came out of this, but certainly some laughs as the model accurately nailed how we saw each other. This process helped to set the context for how each of us may go about approaching the work ahead.

What Does Success Look Like?

We took time to jot down on post-it notes what we felt success should look like for this team and the organization. The instruction was to place our responses on the flipchart to be reviewed later in the process. As everyone was writing, I glanced around the table. Everyone appeared resolute about identifying success factors and expeditiously placed the post-it notes on the flipchart. We were off and running.

Our Strategic Priorities

Next came a pivotal point, the discussion about our five strategic priorities: how we felt about them, their possible relevance from the year before, our team's understanding of them and, most importantly, any recommendations regarding changing them as a team.

To the credit of our CEO, he allowed the individual team member's voices to come through in this process. After a very short amount of deliberation, there were no changes that anyone around the table recommended to our strategic priorities. The team genuinely felt like what the CEO laid out the year prior when he took over was still very relevant and we were on the right track.

At this point, I was feeling confident about digging deeper into the next step. We then took time as a team to discuss our key programs. We knew going in that this was a potential root cause to our workload—this would take some time. This review of the key programs is where the "real work" happened. We each wrote down our key programs by department on post-it notes and put them up on the wall around the room.

We did a 'gallery walk,' a business term describing a walk around the room by the team, allowing each person to review what is on the wall and add their thoughts to the flipcharts via post-it notes and to inquire about items listed by others. This process can ultimately help a team synthesize, rank, and prioritize the items.

As we concluded this process and stepped back and viewed it all, we came to the same realization. Not only was there a lot of work that was in process, there was even more than perhaps any of us had realized until we were able to see it aggregated in this way. This was a critical inflection point that we would come back to on the second day.

Next, we spent time discussing our vision and our mission. We went deep, thinking about the history of the company, the direction that we wanted to take it, and if that required a change in what would show up in our stores and with our teams. The answer there was obvious. We all had an alignment that our vision and mission still fit the culture that we wanted to create in the future.

That may not seem like a big deal, but for any of you that have gone through vision and mission statement exercises, it can be painful. The term wordsmithing usually comes up during the process.

At this point, I felt great. It seemed that the executive team was beginning to have a synergistic feel to it.

We went to dinner that night and continued to bond as a team. What I did not realize was that we had completed the easy part of the work and the day ahead would prove to be much more of a challenge to gain alignment.

How Do We Advance Our Strategy?

The next morning, we arrived ready to take on the day. We picked up where we left off. If our strategy was sound, now it became a discussion about how to get it done faster.

We knew that we needed to advance our strategy. We knew that the strategy was sound, but we also knew that time to execute it was not in our favor. With limited resources, we discussed how to better leverage our teams and even our franchise owners. By the way, we had about eighty employees in total supporting more than 850 stores nationally. True to definition, it was an asset-light model and we were light on assets.

Being a public company presented challenges as well as our ability to invest had to be tempered against shareholder value.

So, to advance the strategy, we knew that we would have to be selective on what we were going to go after. We really had no other choice. That conversation led naturally into a discussion about what might be getting in our way.

Sacred Cows

As day two progressed, we started to make a list of sacred cows— an idea, custom or institution held, (especially unreasonably), to be above criticism.

Sacred cows are those things that are typically protected at all costs regardless of the future direction of the organization. I began to see some cracks in the team when we arrived at this discussion. This discussion of sacred cows is where simplification was starting to be challenged. After all, many of these sacred cows were so embedded that they must not be causing much complexity, right?

What we found was that these sacred cows were, in fact, some of the most complex processes in the company. As the case with most teams discussing sacred cows, it becomes rather easy to rationalize your way through this discussion and do nothing.

We questioned what it would say to our field and headquarters teams if this new executive team ripped out the very fiber of the company.

Oh, I should stop and describe an example of a sacred cow. At Jamba Juice, a sacred cow was the made-to-order Wheatgrass Shot.

The MTO Wheatgrass Shot was a cultural staple at Jamba Juice. It had been a part of the company since the beginning and was a sign of freshness. To watch a team member carefully cut the wheatgrass flat at the proper length and blend it into a two-ounce shot was part of the theater at Jamba Juice. The guests knew that they were receiving 100% goodness.

However, on scale, the MTO Wheatgrass Shot was the most labor-intensive activity in the store. It could take up to four minutes to complete the process of the shot, all for a three-dollar transaction. We did a handful of MTO Wheatgrass Shots per store per day—not enough to drive a significant amount of sales, but enough that we could not take it away without a revolt from our guests and even questions from our team members about eroding our culture.

That was truly a sacred cow... and true to the definition, we did not get rid of the MTO Wheatgrass Shot.

Ultimately, we did not have a lot of traction around making

changes on any sacred cows that day, and you know what, we were okay with that. We were willing to sacrifice this opportunity for simplification by leaving these sacred cows in place. We also learned that we had more sacred cows than we thought, and the process of change was perhaps more complicated than we thought.

Red Herrings

As the morning of the second day progressed, we began to discuss the red herrings of the business—something that is not important and that distracts you from the main subject or problem you're considering. We found it very difficult to identify anything in this space to help with simplification.

As I would learn later, this was a blind spot for the team. In fact, this may have been our most significant collective blind spot. We were so distracted so often that it became our norm, and we simply could not identify and separate the red herrings from our legitimate priorities.

One such red herring was a tea project. We couldn't stun it, we couldn't kill it, and worse, we couldn't even execute it. It had every layer of complexity possible with the smallest amount of payback possible. It was the hottest potato of the hot potatoes. Literally no one wanted this project. A red herring if I ever saw one. It would continue to keep us distracted for months to come.

On this day, we couldn't spend the energy resolving it, although in retrospect, we should have.

Roadblocks

Roadblocks- defined as something that blocks progress or prevents accomplishment of an objective. Well, there were plenty of roadblocks. What we discovered is that most of them were not within our control, so while we had discussion about them, we did not linger, given that there were so many other areas that we needed to discuss.

For example, we identified being a publicly traded company as a roadblock. We knew that being public created a limitation as to what we could invest to turn the business around. We also identified the audit as a roadblock, but obviously something that we had to comply with and indeed had no control over either.

We concluded that a business beyond a turnaround, with a more tenured team, would have lent itself to more examination of roadblocks... but not in the current environment. So, we forged ahead.

Are We Talking To Ourselves?

As we went through this process, this was about identifying things that we interpret differently than others outside of the organization. Said differently, it was a focus on things that we believe are important but that our guests and franchise owners do not care about at all. Perhaps, we had not been facing our realities.

I was pleasantly surprised that we could see these for what they were. Many of them we could laugh about and fortunately acknowledge that their impact was minimal. For the things that we identified worth re-visiting, there was no energy to do so in the short term.

SWOT Analysis

We went through the process to capture our strengths, weaknesses, opportunities, and threats.

The good news was that there were no surprises here. Because the strategic priorities were a result of a SWOT analysis from the prior year, and consistent with our assessment of the strategic priorities, we saw no urgent need to make any changes. We also realized that we either had work in process against the items we listed, or we had agreed when and how we would address them.

This felt like a classic tenet of a business turnaround- we knew what the problems were and how to go after them- we just needed time and resources to do so.

What Will We Say No To?

The next order of business was to contemplate all of what we had discussed during the past two days, evaluate everything that was on each of the flipcharts and address the flipchart on the wall with the question of things we would stop doing.

The conversation around this topic was immediately robust, and there was terrific energy around stopping some of the low-value or low-priority work. As the conversation continued, we challenged every key program on the flipcharts.

There was a compelling reason to stop most of the items on our list, but there seemed just as compelling a reason to continue them. I learned a lot during this process.

I heard a lot of terms like- "Let's let it play out," "let's revisit it in thirty days," "the train has left the station on that one," "we have already invested capital in that one," "this one takes minimal effort to implement."

Yes, that is where this was headed. When the dust settled on the process, as a team, we had not eliminated anything off our list—not one single key program. Every item on the list was justified in some way by someone around the table.

Priority Matrix (Stop/Start/Continue)

That led us to the last flipchart. This exercise was about synthesizing the work into three categories of Start, Stop and Continue. Since we could not agree on anything to stop and we already had plenty of work in process to continue, there was certainly no appetite to add anything new and therefore no need for this part of the exercise.

It was somewhat of an anticlimactic end to the meeting—not in a negative way, just not in a positive way.

In summary, simplification is difficult. Prioritization is even more difficult.

Again, before you can get to prioritization, you must simplify. Attempting to prioritize a large number of initiatives is not a winning strategy. Something will not get focused on and, in fact, some things should not. They should not even be on your list.

As we returned to the office with our message to our teams, we felt a sense of teamwork for sure, but frankly, we struggled for the next few months. Not for lack of effort, but simply because we were in a business turnaround.

While we accomplished a lot of work, we failed at other work and frustrated our teams at times. We stayed in this state of a heavy workload going through this business transformation... until we decided to do another offsite meeting six months later. During that process, we made further progress, but again faced the struggle of attempting to reduce the amount of work. Even when we were effective at eliminating work and solving problems, new problems would surface. It was just the nature of a business transformation.

In reflection, we did not deliver fully on simplification and prioritization in every aspect of the business, but it was quite an accomplishment, all things considered. It gave me a different level of appreciation of what an actual business turnaround looks like and how leaders are challenged to lead through it.

Most complexity originates in strategic planning. Strat planning processes are complicated by design. Many people believe that strategy cannot be simple.

Of course, strategic planning is vital as it informs the entire organization and other stakeholders, but you can also make simplification mandatory. I would say that you must make simplification mandatory in strategic planning. Identifying what teams should stop doing in the coming year is just as critical as outlining what they need to start doing.

CHAPTER *12:*

Indecision

Considering all that I have covered in this book, none of it may matter if you cannot engage and follow through on making decisions.

Let me start with a story.

When former President Ronald Reagan was young, he had an aunt who took him to a cobbler for a pair of new shoes. The cobbler asked the young Ronald Reagan, "Do you want square toes or round toes on your shoes?"

Unable to decide, Reagan did not answer, so the cobbler gave him a few days to think about it. Several days later, the cobbler saw young Reagan on the street and asked him again whether he wanted square toes or round toes on his shoes. Reagan still could not decide, so the shoemaker, with a measure of frustration in his voice, replied, "Well, come by in a couple of days. Your shoes will be ready."

So, a couple of days later, the young Reagan was excited to get his new shoes. When the future president arrived at the cobbler's shop, his shoes were ready, but he found one square-toed shoe and one round-toed shoe!

"This will teach you never to let people make decisions for you," the cobbler said to his indecisive customer. Reagan would later say, "I learned right then and there if you do not make your own decisions, someone else will make them for you."

There are many consequences related to indecision. Perhaps, one that does not always come to the forefront is that if you decide not to decide, you may give up your power of choice. In the case of former President Reagan, it was a painful lesson learned.

Indecision can be as crippling to an organization as any behavior, and it certainly can be to you as a leader. It is one thing not to have alignment on a decision; it is another thing to make a poor decision. But not deciding at all may yield the most significant consequence of all.

Indecision can have an impact on how you are assessed as a leader and can ultimately be a factor in whether people want to follow you at all. The term "that's why they pay you the big bucks" has been said many times by employees talking about their leaders. The intimation is that you're paid to make decisions, so make them... even if they're difficult decisions.

Indecision can be an illusion, though. Indecision can imply that we are unable to decide. However:

Even when you are not making a decision, you are deciding not to make a decision.

This action is an important distinction. The precious time that you are wasting, and the brain cells that you're utilizing while not making the decision is still costing you mental energy. You will eventually need to exert more brain cells and time to make the decision that you did not make already.

What I have observed are examples of indecision that show up in all areas of society.

For example, the Minnesota Vikings (a football team in the NFL), were "on-the-clock" to pick a player in the 2003 NFL Draft. "On-the-clock" means that it was their turn to draft a player and the process allows for a set amount of time before the next team in order has the opportunity on-the-clock to select a player.

Football teams generally spend most of the year thinking about specific players that they want to draft for the upcoming year to become a part of their team and when their time comes to make a selection, they choose the players that appear to be the best fit for their organization. Of course, this is assuming that those players are still available in the draft when their time comes to make a selection.

Team executives not only know which players they want to draft, they likely know who teams picking near them are looking to recruit as well. To that point, teams are typically prepared with contingency picks, if the player that they intended to choose is no longer available.

To the average person, having most of the year to think this through and then fifteen minutes "on-the-clock" to make the selection seems like plenty of time.

Having gone through all of this and with all the resources available to them, the 2003 Vikings still ran out of time when it was their turn to make a selection.

It wasn't just that the Vikings could not decide which player to select. To complicate matters, at the last minute the Vikings were listening to offers from three other teams looking to trade up to pick a player sooner—the Baltimore Ravens, the Jacksonville Jaguars, and the New England Patriots. With about thirty seconds remaining out of the fifteen minutes that the Vikings had to make their pick, the Vikings officials claim that they submitted their draft card requesting a trade with Baltimore to acquire the Ravens' first, fourth and sixth-round picks (the Ravens were picking three spots later than the Vikings in the first round of the draft). League officials, however, told the Vikings that they never received verification of the trade from Ravens' officials.

At this point, the clock had run out on the Vikings, making it possible for teams picking after them to swoop in and make their pick before Minnesota could. The Jacksonville Jaguars took quarterback Byron Leftwich, the player who the Ravens were allegedly trading up to obtain.

In the ensuing chaos, another team was also able to make their selection before the Vikings were able to finally select a player.

Even after slipping two spots in the first round, the Vikings still wound up selecting Kevin Williams, a defensive tackle who played for them for eleven years, making the Pro Bowl five times as one of the best players at his position. From that perspective, the pick seemed to work out despite all the confusion.

The Vikings version of the story asserts that Kevin Williams was the player that they wanted to draft all along. Even if that was the case, it was still an embarrassing situation and a demonstration of how indecision can happen anywhere to anyone at any time.

Another example of the impact of indecision: There is a joke about 'Buridan's Donkey.' Aristotle originally formulated it, but it was popularized by the French philosopher, Jean Buridan. The joke is as follows...

A hungry donkey walks into a barn. In the barn, there are two equally large and inviting bales of straw. They are also both equally visible and accessible. The donkey dies of starvation.

Buridan's Donkey implies that when you find yourself caught between what appears to be two equally attractive options, the worst course of action is to choose neither. Indecision.

It may be an exaggerated example of indecision, but even the persistence of an undecided state for a perceptible length of time may be a relative "death" regarding the situation that requires a decision that you are just not making.

I love this joke, but indecision is no laughing matter for many of us, and indecision may be occurring in our lives more often than we realize.

There is a paradoxical aspect of this joke that I must acknowledge, which is that you could argue that no two choices are exactly alike. There is always some factor that can differentiate the two choices. If it is possible at all to distinguish between things, those things must not be exactly alike.

First, remember that it is a joke intended to poke fun at the topic of indecision. Second, back to my approach to this book—I'm focusing more on pragmatism than I am academia. However, let me address this:

To the human brain, yes if two choices appear to be the same, then the point is that you are not able, in that moment, to define what is different in the available options. Therefore, not making one more desirable than the other to choose causes indecision.

However, thankfully for us, the brain is not so simplistic. If the only factor governing a choice were a mathematical evaluation, then two possible outcomes with the same evaluation could result in inaction. However, most of the decisions that we make every day have nothing to do with mathematical equations.

We could even say that choice only happens with an unequal evaluation of possible outcomes. And to the extent that your brain does act, we can conclude its assessment of reasonable alternatives were unequal. Enter cognitive gifts that we have been given, like intuition.

So, if the mind can differentiate that the options available are unequal, then why are we so indecisive at times and how can we understand it better?

Obviously, the answer may not be the same for all of us, but here are a few possible reasons for you to explore:

- Anxiety About Making The Wrong Decision
- Afraid Of Failure
- Worry About What Others Will Think Of You
- Overanalyzing The Situation
- Wanting The Perfect Solution
- Absence Of Trust
- Procrastination

Anxiety About Making The Wrong Decision

Anxiety about making the wrong decision is one of the most common reasons that people hesitate when faced with a choice.

Bruno, a friend of mine, is a psychiatrist (no, not mine!) He explained anxiety to me with such clarity many years ago that it has stuck with me. He contrasted fear and anxiety. Bruno explained that it was important to do so because, often in our lives, we confuse fear with anxiety. He acknowledged that there is a fine line between fear and anxiety and that they are similar and feel similar.

If we believe our anxious moments are fear, we may likely overemphasize the situation and respond in a more uncharacteristic way than we otherwise should respond. This is how Bruno explained the difference:

Well, of course, the clinical differences first: Fear is an emotional reaction to a perceived imminent and dangerous threat. It is accompanied by a host of other feelings such as horror or sadness and typically invokes the "fight-or-flight" response, wherein the person feeling fear either responds to the fear by confronting it or by running from and escaping it.

Anxiety is a response to a potential future event. Anxiety is an emotional state usually characterized by worry, inner turmoil, and nervousness. It is common for anxious people not to know what the source of their anxiety is, and in some cases, it does not even have a source. Anxiety can strongly affect a person's behavior and negatively affect their ability to go about their daily lives.

Now the practical difference: Bruno said that if you are standing in a glass room with a lion on the outside of the room watching you, this is anxiety. To be clear, the door is locked, and the glass is shatterproof. The lion cannot get in. Even being equipped with this information may not make you feel much better, but you are not actually in harm's way. Anxiety is that you see the lion, and you are worried about what could happen, but you are safe inside the glass room. Anxiety is the manifestation of everything that could go wrong and genuinely believing that it is going to go wrong.

Fear is different- fear is... the lion is now in the glass room with you.

Fear is a more imminent danger, not just the prospect of what could happen if everything went wrong, but a much higher probability that something will go wrong.

Anxiety is not an imminent danger, but your mind can take

you to that place of worry, even though the implications of the situation are not that grave.

I apologize for the digression, but this distinction was a valuable lesson for me, not just in my personal life, but even for making decisions in the boardroom.

I can apply this to many situations in business when I allowed anxiety to turn into fear and did not make the decisions that I needed to make, right or wrong.

All this to say, it is not unnatural to be anxious about decisions that we must make, but if we elevate them to fear, it may change the way that we think about making decisions and potentially increase our probability of indecision.

So, sensing the anxiety of making the wrong decision, it is okay to ask yourself what is the worst that can happen as a result of my choice? However, you owe it to yourself to also ask what is the best that can occur as a result of my decision?

In doing so, you may be able to manage your anxiety when it comes to making decisions and prevent it from elevating to a level of fear.

Afraid Of Failure

Failure can stop the best of us in our tracks. After all, none of us want to fail. The risk of deciding and not being successful as a result of the decision can be a significant contributor to future indecision.

The first thing you must tell yourself is that failure is always a potential consequence of decisions that you make. It does not mean that you will fail, and it does not mean that you won't fail, but acknowledging the risk may help. The pessimist may look at that and say it is only fifty-fifty odds. The optimist will look at the situation and believe that they have just as much opportunity to get it right as they do wrong. They both can be right... or they both can be wrong.

Being afraid of failure when it comes to making decisions is not a numbers game. It is about taking inventory of what you know, what you have learned, and what your intuition tells you about what could happen- all aspects are essential.

History is littered with examples of failures that later turned into successes at all levels of society. There are well-publicized examples like Thomas Edison and so many other inventors, business leaders, even U.S. Presidents. Some also believe that failure is a prerequisite to success, that it is almost impossible to get anything right the first time that you do it or make a decision about it.

Think back to the first time that you attempted to skate or ride a bike or hit a baseball. Unless you are gifted in some way different from the rest of us on planet earth, the first time attempting any of those activities likely did not go well. It took practice. Decision-making also takes practice. And with practice comes failure.

In a business role, I can remember the first time that I wrote a work schedule... and didn't get it right. The first performance review that I delivered... and didn't do it well. The first person that I promoted and... well, I may not have gotten that right either.

So, being afraid to fail is one area in which you must give yourself a break. You are likely going to make some decisions that you would like to take back... but don't spend the energy and time there. Acknowledge it; others will appreciate that level of vulnerability. Then make a great decision the next time.

Worried About What Others Will Think Of You?

I have learned that the human psyche is far more fragile than perhaps we sometimes realize. It is interesting when I hear someone say that they do not care what other people think about them. Maybe the question needs to be posed to understand who those other people are that they're talking about. Perhaps, we genuinely do not care about what strangers think. Or we don't care about those who don't factor into the course of our day-to-day lives. That is very different than saying that you don't care what those close to you think about you—your significant other, parents, children, siblings or those outside of your family that can have a direct impact on your life, like your boss.

The human psyche needs connection: to be wanted, to be needed, to be accepted, to be loved- some of us just need it to a more considerable degree than others, based on many life factors.

So, the point of this is, worrying about what others think

regarding the decisions that we make is more common than not, even for those who will not admit that it matters to them.

Remember though, in the context of business and being in a leadership role, you are responsible for making decisions. It is easy for others to second-guess your decisions or be critical of them in the aftermath, but if you have acted in good faith with the decision that you made, you should focus less on what others think.

Overanalyzing The Situation

Many people who have trouble making decisions may tend to overanalyze a decision. There comes a time when no matter how much information you have, or how much logic that you have applied, the decision isn't going to get any easier and the choices aren't going to get any better.

Most people know someone that they work with who is highly analytical, possibly to a fault. Many times, the position we hold in an organization can influence how cautious we are in making decisions. However, overanalyzing the situation can happen to anyone, personally or professionally.

Waiting for just one more piece of data can be tempting. It may reveal something new that influences the decision that you make. It can be tricky, though, as many decisions are time-bound and the luxury of continuing to wait usually does not exist.

This is not to say trust your instinct on every decision. Instincts can be a result of all the personal experiences that we have amassed, and for the decision at hand, it could be useless if you have no knowledge or experience related to the decision needed.

Overanalyzing a decision can also be a result of the one time that you trusted your instinct and the situation did not go so well. You may have planted somewhere in your subconscious that you will never let that happen again... and you don't. You ensure that no future decisions will be made in haste. The problem with this is that not all decisions are the same. You may be holding out on making somewhat simple decisions due to your need to be safe and evaluate all information.

There is yet another component to overanalyzing. Fact-checking. You may end up further aggravating the situation by needing to fact check the data. Fact-checking is a real symptom of overanalyzing the situation. You have data that supports your decision, but you don't trust it, so you get more data to validate the data that you already have. You can see how this can take you down a rabbit hole. More time equates to more indecision. Back to the discussion about being afraid of failure in decision-making.

The more you practice, the greater the likelihood of making better future decisions. So is the case with finding the balance between data and intuition. With practice, you should find confidence to move forward in deciding with some level of data versus the need for all the data.

Wanting The Perfect Solution

Perfectionism may be getting in your way.

I spent a good portion of my professional life being a (frustrated) perfectionist. Perhaps my family would tell me that behavior has not been limited to just my professional life. I realized over time that I did not necessarily make a better decision because I took more time to decide and the anguish over the decision that I made did not diminish at all because I thought it through for a more extended period. Pulling the proverbial trigger was always challenged with the risk of the decision being somehow deficient.

Perfectionism can have an impact on so many aspects of our lives. Anyone who has obsessive-compulsive disorder (OCD) or know someone that does, are aware it can be crippling. Some would equate perfectionism to OCD—there are definite similarities. OCD is the urge to repeat an activity over and over until it is just right. For someone with OCD, straightening a can on a shelf can take two to three minutes because of the need to reposition it repeatedly until it is just right. A perfectionist may not go quite that far, but the feeling of being unfulfilled with a decision can lead to not making a decision until everything is "just right" ... which may never happen.

Some of our perfectionism beliefs and behaviors are self-inflicted.

Here is what I mean- we say things like "Give it 110%." Wow, 100% of anything would be incredible. You could say this is just a figure of speech. To that, I say words matter. Creating an environment in which you expect perfection, or aim beyond perfection with the 110% moniker, intentional or not, can create the unintended consequence that people believe their effort and work output is never good enough. As a result, they will continue to work toward perfection, as though it is achievable, only to be frustrated in the end.

As it relates to decision-making, perfectionism can have that same impact. A decision cannot be made until everything is according to plan. Maybe the decision that you haven't made is what is preventing everything from going according to plan.

I don't mean to poke fun at this serious topic but do make the decision. You have a responsibility to continually assess how your decisions as a leader impact the environment around you — in this case, not making a decision.

Even terms like the pursuit of perfection can be dangerous. It is a bit more of an indirect term but likely leaves you in the same place. It works well in a luxury car commercial, but not so much in real life. Words matter so be careful how they work into your conversations and, more importantly, into your actions.

This may sound like accepting less than 100% is okay. I do not suspect most people set out to make poor decisions or to be unsuccessful in general. However, effective leadership means striking a balance between taking risks and providing consistent, steady leadership. Perfectionism does not allow the space for risks.

In the end, as it relates to decision-making, we cannot often wait for the perfect situation; in fact, almost never.

Absence Of Trust

Indecision can also befall those who lack trust, either in others, in the work that they are doing, or even in themselves.

There was a story about three brothers, Jack, Robert, and John, who decided to go on a picnic. They'd been planning this for weeks, ever since school had let out for summer. But their father kept them so busy with work around the farm that this was the first opportunity to get away.

Jack packed sandwiches, Robert gathered the drinks and John, being the youngest of the three brothers, just tagged along. As they headed off into the woods, about halfway to their destination, it started to rain, so they took shelter under a large tree and began talking among themselves.

Given the arrangement of the clouds, it looked like the rain was there to stay. Determined to continue with their picnic plans, the two older brothers, Jack and Robert, turned to John and said, "Look, we made the sandwiches, we brought the drinks, and you brought nothing, so you should be the one to go home and get the umbrellas. Get the umbrellas and meet us back here. We will continue into the woods, and then we'll have our picnic."

Of course, being the younger brother, John was often picked on by his older brothers, so he naturally had a suspicion about his brothers' motives. John, showing no sign of intimidation, said, "You must be joking. As soon as I'm around the corner you're going to eat the food, you're going to drink the drinks, and when I come back with the umbrellas, there will be nothing left."

Jack and Robert said, "We will do no such thing." John said, "You absolutely will. There is no way I am doing that."

Eventually, the older brothers convinced John that they would not have the picnic until he comes back with the umbrellas.

So, John left. Minutes went by. Minutes became hours and hours became days. On the third day, Jack turns to Robert and said, "I'm really hungry, it's been way too long. How about it, why don't we just eat the sandwiches and drink the drinks?"

As soon as Jack said this, a voice from behind a rock said, "If you do, I will not go and get the umbrellas!"

What is the moral of the story? Well, it involves an absence of trust. John did not trust his brothers and, in the end, a great deal of time was wasted by John hiding behind the rock, and nothing was accomplished.

Absence of trust in yourself making a decision can be problematic as it can make you second-guess your approach. Not only does it have the potential of slowing down your decision, but you may not even like the decision that you finally make.

Absence of trust can be traced back to your discomfort in the role that you are in, unfamiliarity with the material or situation requiring a decision, or even muscle memory of trusting yourself regarding a prior decision and not liking the outcome.

Absence of trust can be outward to others as well. You may not believe that others involved in the decision or impacted by the decision will deliver on what they need to do. This, in turn, can affect your decision.

For example, you need to stay late at work to finish a project due the next day, and you need your son in high school to pick up his younger brother from afterschool practice. Your older son is notoriously forgetful, though. So, what do you do? Do you leave work and compromise your time to get the project complete or do you trust that your son will deliver this time?

Back to muscle memory. It can be challenging to make a decision against what your mind tells you will happen the next time, based on the last time. To be the most efficient decision-maker that you can be, it will be important to demonstrate trust in all dimensions.

Procrastination

One of the most significant impacts of indecision is the time that we waste, and during that time of procrastination, the situation could become even more challenging or change in a way that requires new choices to be considered to make the decision. And this consumes even more time. You can see how this can become a cyclical problem.

Procrastination is a concern that needs to be addressed simply because it can become a habit of constantly taking more time than required. This can allow any one of these previously mentioned reasons to escalate—you begin to overanalyze, worry about failing, etc.

There are many reasons why we procrastinate.

A lack of structure can cause procrastination. One solution is to engineer your environment in a way that makes your desired goal more likely to happen.

Many years ago, I had an administrative assistant that worked with me, and she always spent time talking to the nanny that babysat her six and seven-year-old children. She was so worried that she would sometimes spend fifteen to twenty minutes at a time on the phone with the nanny giving instruction, multiple times a day. All the while, I would reach a boiling point due to the lack of productivity. As I learned over time, it was more about her simply putting work off until later. She believed that it should not matter as long as the work was completed at the end of the day.

To address that, I began to frontload her work, specifically my requests of her in the first four hours of the day and put deadlines to get it done before she left for lunch. It dramatically reduced the amount of time that she was on the phone, but it also made the work timebound, reducing the amount of time for procrastination.

Perhaps, the most significant predictor of procrastination is a task that is considered undesirable. These could include routine activities like cleaning or doing the laundry. It is human nature to want to replace something that we do not want to do with something that we love to do, almost ensuring procrastination. Decision-making is no different. It is easier to shift your focus to decisions that are easy or related to something that you will enjoy.

Procrastination is delaying... what is undoubtedly inevitable. Again, while you are procrastinating, the situation may be evolving, and when you finally step up to make the decision, it may not be the right one because of the time-lapse and the changing conditions.

It is unlikely that the need to make a decision is going to go away so you might as well stop procrastinating and make the decision... before the next decision that you need to make comes along.

You may find that the more you can identify and eliminate the reasons for indecision, the better your decisions and choices are. Not only do you get a better result, but you also reap other benefits, like saving time.

CHAPTER 13:

Putting It All Together

So, let me tie this together.

In chapter one, I shared my experience working with the consultants who used the phrase The Power Of And. I also shared my visceral reaction to it. In part, that engagement shaped the overall narrative of this book and of course, the title. However, with everything that I have shared, I have only represented the professional motivation for writing this book.

There is also a personal story to this journey.

I have carried around the idea of writing this book for years. The business side of the story has always been compelling, but apparently not compelling enough on its own to move me to write the book. If so, the book would have been written many years ago. Even if I had said out loud to those close to me that writing the book was a priority, which I did, my actions did not meet up with my words.

And so, week after week, month after month, and year after year, I carried around the notes and outline for this book. I carried them on every flight and added a line or two, and if I was really in a creative mood, I wrote a whole page while in the air. Writing the book was always top-of-mind as I would use any idle time to add to the story, but it obviously wasn't quite high enough on the priority list.

There were many barriers to completing the book, real or perceived. Time was certainly one of them, perhaps the biggest barrier. Time was my enemy... and time was winning.

Then it happened, I was given the greatest gift that I could receive... not the one that comes from family and friends as they frantically search every year during the holidays or on my birthday to find something for me that I don't already have. That is usually a futile exercise, but I appreciate their effort just the same.

No, nothing material.

I was given the gift of time.

Jamba Juice was bought by Focus Brands, my COO role ended, and my severance package was activated. The ability to take a year or two off at this stage of my career was now a reality.

The barrier of time had been eliminated. It was time to thread the life and professional experiences together to tell this story.

What was meant to be a leisure year off from work beginning in late 2018 through 2019, after leaving my role at Jamba Juice, has been nothing of the sort.

I called this my "gap" year. My children, who are currently in college, laughed at that one. I don't usually demonstrate comedic talents, but I have my moments.

Of course, with the time off, I was planning to travel, but in a way that I could enjoy the cities and truly relax. Well, I did get to travel, but not to the level that I had envisioned.

I had also planned to create my own business providing consulting, coaching, public speaking and publishing services. Well, actually I did accomplish that. In reflection, I am not sure how I did it. Let me explain why.

During my last month with Jamba Juice, I decided to fly from Frisco back to Austin and play basketball at the gym with my youngest son. We were finally getting a gym membership together and the basketball court staring back at us through the glass front frame was the motivation.

We signed up on the first Saturday morning in October. After completing all the necessary paperwork, we went immediately to the basketball court. With this gym being new to the community, people were still discovering the location. To that point, the gym wasn't very busy yet and, on that day, we were the only two people on the basketball court. The opportunity for us to play one-on-one had been building for months and knowing that I was going to be off from work for a year or more, this would be the first of many battles to come... or so we thought.

I checked the ball up to my son and the game began. We had not been playing five minutes when I slipped and fell. I landed awkwardly on my left arm and I knew right away that something was wrong. It may seem odd to hear, but I was hoping for a broken arm- bones can heal much faster than tendons. Instead, I had torn my left tricep. In all my years of participating in sports, I had repeatedly said that there are only two injuries I never wanted to experience-a torn achilles or a tricep tear. What are the odds? It seemed as though the universe was against me.

Fortunately, there was a hospital right across the street. Even at the time I thought that was odd and really convenient. Maybe it is big business for hospitals to locate near gyms understanding that injuries will likely occur in the gym environment.

At the hospital, they performed tests to determine the severity of the injury. There were many things that went through my head at that time, but ironically pain was not one of them. On a scale of 1-10, the pain level was only a three, so I forged on. With the surgeon receiving the imaging in a couple of days, I flew back to Frisco and went back to work on Monday morning.

After the surgeon reviewed the imaging, he called me on Wednesday, four days after the injury, to discuss. It was determined that I needed surgery right away. The surgeon shared with me that my lack of pain had little to do with my personal toughness. It was more a result of all the tendons being torn off the bone, so in effect there was nothing left to cause much pain. Rehab, and plenty of it, was in my immediate future.

The injury was mostly devastating because of the surprise of it.

I had not had a major injury in more than twenty-five years. The injury slowed me down physically for sure, but it also slowed me down mentally... and not in a good way. For someone who was always in constant motion, stopping work and having surgery at the same time was a bad combination. I had too much time to think. The injury just seemed so random and yet, it turned out to be more of a marker for what was to come in the next few months.

Only a few weeks later, our family dog, Gino, passed away at the age of 14. You must understand- Gino was more than a dog. Gino was as close to being human without being human. Those of you that have dogs, and especially those that have had a dog pass away, understand this feeling.

Gino was a five-pound Pomeranian that looked like a stuffed toy. With his little brown eyes, all he had to do was look at us and he got anything that he wanted.

Gino spent many days laying on my office desk next to me while I took conference calls. Gino also spent a lot of time being carried over my shoulder- he was my guy. This is where my life situations begin to converge. Because of the recovery needed for my arm, I was unable to reach down and pick Gino up for the last few weeks of his life.

It is often said that time heals all wounds. That may be true, but in this situation, time has not caught up yet.

Perhaps the most difficult decision to make after losing a dog is when to get another dog. It usually has to do with your level of pain. Well, I am still not there more than a year later...

Only a couple of weeks after losing Gino, our youngest son, Christian, suffered a major seizure and almost died. It was the morning of New Year's Day.

Christian had declared his resolutions for the new year. Christian had even taken time to ask us for our resolutions. He was in good spirits. We didn't see this coming.

I turned and went out the front door for a walk. Only a couple of minutes later, I received a frantic call on my cell phone to return to the house. Christian was still experiencing the seizure when I walked in but had suffered through the worst parts of it. Unfortunately, my wife was there to experience it all. We spent the rest of the day at the emergency room with Christian trying to understand what had happened and why.

After much testing and appointments, Christian was deemed to have a low risk of a repeat seizure. Nonetheless, Christian could not drive to and from work because of the requirements after having a seizure so I became his personal chauffeur for the next few weeks and months. Christian's seizure was a very difficult way to start the year.

All the while, my mother was dying from a horrible disease called PLS. Primary lateral sclerosis is a rare neuromuscular disease characterized by progressive muscle weakness in the voluntary muscles. This disease robs you of every quality of life- walking, talking, all motor skills- she needed complete 24-hour care. I don't wish for anyone to have to experience what my mother went through or experience what I had to witness her going through.

As a family, we had celebrated my mother's 75th birthday with her in August. It was a rare occasion, that my sister, my brother and most of our children were together, but this was a big occasion and a big milestone. My mother's condition was clearly deteriorating, but she made it to 75 and was still able to communicate with us and enjoy it. That would be the last time that we would visit her as a family- it was just too difficult after that.

In fact, from Halloween on, most of my visits consisted of just me going and sitting with my mother and trying to interpret her needs as she was no longer able to talk. Thanksgiving was difficult, the Christmas visit was even more difficult. On both occasions, I fed her and talked to her. That was all that I could do.

By New Year's Day, I could see an accelerated deterioration in her condition. There was nothing that anyone could do. With every visit, I tried to be positive and strong for my mother and, for the most part, I would demonstrate strength as I sat with her. Upon leaving the facility, every visit ended with me sitting in my car and crying... every time.

I felt helpless, the situation felt unfair and there was absolutely no way for me to take anything positive from it. It was the toughest of tough times.

I would make my final visit to see my mother the weekend of March 1st, 2nd and 3rd after being away for a couple of weeks. I could not believe how much that she had changed. I knew, in that moment, that the end was near.

There was a small radio next to my mother's pillow that was playing verses from the bible. My sister had sent it a few weeks earlier and asked the staff to play this for my mother. The room had the feeling of finality. I sat with her for an hour or so, but there was a feeling of her not even being there- physically yes, but in spirit, no. She had no eye movement, no sounds and no reaction to anything that I said or did. I was numb. I left with a feeling of shock and a reality that I had not experienced on any visit before.

I suppose that part of me believed that no matter how devastating her situation, she would be there forever, even in that condition. It was not right for me to want that, but I knew how strong her will was to live.

I returned the next day, on Saturday afternoon. To my surprise, she was alert. She saw me, her eyes followed me, and she even smiled twice- once when she saw me and once in response to my wife's voice over the phone telling her a funny story. It was a small miracle and you know what, just what I needed. While I still left and went to cry in my car, I had something to hold onto. At this stage of her life, I would take anything positive.

I returned on Sunday afternoon. Unfortunately, my mother had returned to the condition that she was in on Friday. My heart sank. I knew that this was the end. I knew that this would be the last time that I would see her alive. I said everything that I wanted to say to her.

I went outside and cried in my car for the last time.

My sister flew into town that Sunday as I was leaving town. She called me on Tuesday afternoon to tell me that our mother had passed away.

I can say that there is nothing like losing your mother-no disrespect to my father.

The gift of time allowed me to spend time with my mother that I would not have spent if I were still working. I am thankful to Focus Brands and their leaders for coming into the picture and purchasing Jamba Juice when they did. In most business deals like this, you are making a case to find a way to stay in role. Not me, I was thankful for being given an opportunity to exit the role.

Oh, and one more thing. Tucked in between the timeline of my son's seizure and my mother passing away, my father was placed in a medically induced coma for seventeen days… after I saved his life. True story.

The context of that is this… my father and I did not have an adversarial relationship-we just didn't have a relationship at all. My parents divorced when I was four years old, I lived with my father for one year when I was fifteen and I have seen him intermittently every few years at family reunions.

Other than that, I spent the rest of my childhood living with my mother. Growing up I was never abused by my parents, but I was neglected. They were both raised by parents that didn't invest a lot of time in each of them. Well, my mother being one of thirteen children and my father being one of ten children probably had something to do with that. I have come to realize in my journey that there are "Benefits Of Neglect." That is a topic for another book.

So, it is early January, only days after my son's seizure. I called my father and told him that I was coming to visit him. He said okay. It was a bit odd because we did not do any catching up on the phone. It was a very short call. That alone made the visit expectation a bit more ominous. Truly, this visit could go really, really bad or really, really good.

Admittedly, I had been angry at my father for years, but I didn't really know what I was angry about. Of course, the obvious things like not being a part of my life, not reaching out to me, not knowing my family, not knowing my accomplishments, etc. I felt robbed of something and I didn't know who to blame or how to handle it, so I blamed him. Until I realized that I had just as much of the blame to shoulder as he did.

Back to this visit. I didn't want my hostility to carry into our visit, but I also didn't want to miss the opportunity to ask him tough questions that I had been carrying for years.

My trip to visit my dad in Louisville, Kentucky was on for early February.

The first day that I arrived, I checked into the hotel and immediately went to his apartment on the 17th floor. We spent three hours sitting and talking- it was the first time that I had been alone with him in a room in thirty-five years!

The visit could not have gone any better. Our conversation ended with my father asking me to come back the following morning to make breakfast. I realized that there would be a time for tough questions, but this wasn't it.

I returned the following morning at 9:00 a.m. I did notice that my father had been coughing the night before and by the next morning, the cough was much more pronounced. For someone that I have spent very little time around but knowing that he has been a heavy drinker most of his life, the cough was not a total surprise... and he was 81 years old. In addition to the coughing, I noticed around 10:00 a.m. that he was falling back to sleep as we talked. Again, at 81 years old, waking up at 4:00 a.m. probably precipitates a nap at 10:00 a.m.

After a few minutes of the cough drowning out our conversation and his constant nodding, I told him that I would come back later.

I left and visited other relatives that I had not seen in years and it ended up being a productive and much needed day for me personally. I called my father that evening on my return to town. I asked him if he needed anything or if he wanted me to come by. He said no but come in the morning and we will try breakfast again. I said okay and headed to the hotel. I went to bed rather early that night- earlier than usual and early given that I was in a later time zone than where I live.

Because of the early turn-in, I heard my phone ringing at 5:50 a.m. the next morning. It was my father. He asked me to call my cousin who looks after him. He stated that he needed her to take him to the clinic. He didn't know her phone number, which was odd since they talked almost every other day. In fact, he didn't know anyone's phone number. I had to call my Aunt that has everyone's contact.

I hung up with my father and called my cousin- no answer. I called her brother- no answer. I called my father back and shared my inability to reach my cousin. I asked him if he wanted me to take him to the clinic and he responded by saying, "no, please call 9-1-1."

I don't know my father well, but I know him well enough to know that is not something that he would say. I called 9-1-1 and immediately drove to my father's apartment. I met the paramedics in the lobby, and we went up to the 17th floor together. I was very nervous about what we were going to find. Fortunately, the door was unlocked. I found my father in the bathroom. He was getting dressed- jeans, belt and all. The paramedics sat him down and began to take vitals. He was immediately whisked away to the hospital. I followed and arrived in the emergency room to meet the admitting physician.

The physician had many questions for me that I could not answer. I am sure the doctor thought it was a bit odd- I am his son with same name and I look just like him and know nothing about his medical history. Well, that was the situation.

They admitted him and immediately began running tests- a lot of test. I left for a couple of hours to process what had just happened and then returned to the hospital. Upon my return, I was greeted by the attending physician, who said that my father was very lethargic that morning. His CO_2 level was that of sitting in a parked, running car in a closed-in garage. He said two more hours in that condition and my father would not be alive.

Wow, that hit me hard. The physician said that my father had so many medical issues that they didn't know where to start. To address it all, they would need to put my father in a medically-induced coma... it lasted for seventeen days!

I stayed in town for a couple of more days after my father was admitted, but honestly, I did not want to see him die on my watch, after all this time of being disconnected from him.

The good news is that my father did pull through and, at the same time, got the care that he had been desperately needing.

Also, more good news is that the next time I would see my father would be only four weeks later. However, the bad news is that was when I returned to Kentucky with my mother's body to have her funeral in her hometown. Again, another example of my life issues converging.

I visited with my father after the funeral and he looked amazing!

I did have one burning question for him on that visit. It had nothing to do with the issues that I had been storing up over the years. This question was more relevant to the current situation. I asked him, "considering your condition, how did you call me that morning when you went to the hospital?" He replied, "I was so confused and lethargic that I could not remember anyone's phone number, I couldn't even logically think to dial 9-1-1." He went on to say, "the only thing that I could do was press the last number called button and because you had called me the night before, it dialed you and I am fortunate that you answered..."

The next thing that he said caught me completely off guard. He said, "... and you saved my life."

For a son that didn't know for sure if his father even loved him or cared about him for years, this was as extreme as it gets. The emotion that I experienced was unlike any other.

So, there you have it and yes, everything that I have shared happened in the first six months of my time off.

Fortunately, the following six months were not as chaotic. That was good since I still needed time to process everything that had happened in the first six months as there was literally no time to process one situation before the next one arrived.

So, spending time Choosing And Doing What Matters Most, took on a different meaning for me personally in this past year. It was no longer about prioritizing work, then family and friends or even thinking about how I would handle it when I did return to work. No, it was me playing defense with life.

This takes me back to discipline, choices, prioritization. I would like to believe that I would have been as present and as attentive to each of these situations if I had been working at the time. Honestly, I know better than to believe that. Work had been prioritized ahead of everything else. There are a lot of reasons why, but I suppose, at the end of the day, none of them are good enough. I know that, we all know that.

It is likely that I would not have been there to spend time with my mother before she was gone, I would not have been there the day my son had his seizure, I would not have been there the day my dog passed away, and I certainly would not have had the time or made the time to randomly call up my father and go visit him… and ultimately save his life.

So, I share all of this to frame up my state-of-mind for writing this book. Prioritizing your life is not something that you do in the future, it is something that you do now, today.

Time is very precious. Spending unproductive time multitasking, making trivial choices all day and responding to every ding in your life is one way to live, but can you live that way and still be present for what matters most in your life? And if those things matter most, that is your choice. If they are truly not important to you, then don't ignore the human beings, familiar or unfamiliar, that are around you every day.

Only you can answer that question for you, but I hope that my journey shared in this book provides some insight that will help you find that answer.

Demonstrating self-discipline, saying no when you know that you should say no, eliminating multitasking. These are not game-changing concepts, but they create game-changing results if you implement them in your life.

Don't try to do it all. Others will test you, but you must believe in the Power Of Or and demonstrate conviction in your choices, decisions, and priorities that will shape the leader and person that you want to be.

Finally, give yourself a break when it comes to making decisions... but ultimately, make them and be okay with the result.

After all, we all want to choose and do what matters most in our life, so do it.